MASTER YOUR MIND

Build a Resilient Mindset, Gain Mental Clarity, Overcome Overthinking, and Live the Life with Confidence and Freedom

By

Arvind Kaiwartya

Copyright © 2025 by Arvind Kaiwartya

All rights reserved. No part of this book may be reproduced in any form without permission in writing from the author.

No part of this publication may be reproduced or transmitted in any form or by any means, mechanical or electronic, including photocopying or recording , or by any information storage and retrieval system, or transmitted by email or by any other means whatsoever without permission in writing from author.

ACKNOWLEDGMENTS

Any accomplishment requires diligent effort of many people and writing a book is not different.

It is my esteemed pleasure and privilege to share my deep sincere thanks and gratitude to all those who helped me during the journey of my book writing.

First and foremost, I am very thankful to God, who made me meet to my Mentor Mr.Som Bathla Sir.

I would like to express my sincere thanks to my Mentor Mr. Som Sir without his guidance, it was not possible. I thank him for lending me his valuable time, suggestion, and his outstanding session that has enlightened my path of book writing.

Special thanks to Mr. Ravi Tewari Sir for his full support, care, cooperativeness and encouragement and helped me to find solution of every problem.

My acknowledgement cannot be completed without expressing thanks to all my teachers and I am deeply indebted to my family for their blessings, outpouring love, and unfailingly support.

I am very thankful to the editor and publisher whose diligent effort made this publication possible.

Many examples, stories, anecdotes are the result of a collection from various sources such as many books, magazine, newspaper, online sources and some real life experiences. Regardless of the source, I wish to express my gratitude to those who may have contributed to this work, even though anonymously.

At last once again I thank to God for giving me such a wonderful opportunity of book writing and transform the life of people. You have given me your blessing.

Thank you God for everything.

DEDICATION

I dedicate this book to you, the reader. May you apply the life's experience, practical exercise and some special techniques you discover within the book to overcome mind obstacles for long term mental peace. This brings a difference in the lives of all those around you.

This is also dedicated to my family, my teachers, my friends and all entire my well – wishers.

I love you all.

WHY IS THIS BOOK FOR YOU?

"When the mind won't stop, let the soul speak."

Do you find yourself trapped in endless loops of thought, questioning every decision, overanalyzing every word, and mentally revisiting moments long gone?

Master Your Mind takes you deep into the inner world of overthinking—a place where silence is loud, and clarity feels distant.

This book is more than just a guide; it's a mirror for your mind.

Blending the insights of psychology, philosophy, and spirituality, Master Your Mind explores the hidden roots of overthinking and its quiet impact on your emotions, relationships, and purpose. Through rich case studies, modern struggles, real-world examples, and practical tools, this book helps you understand why your mind races—and how to slow it down.

Each chapter gently guides you from mental chaos to clarity, from anxious loops to grounded awareness. Whether you're overwhelmed by digital distractions, emotional overload, or the fear of making the wrong choice, this book speaks to your struggle—and offers a way through.

Inside this book, you'll discover:

- The science and psychology behind overthinking

- Real-life stories that reveal the emotional cost of overanalysis

- Tools to recognize and break free from mental traps

- Daily practices to cultivate peace, clarity, and confidence

- A path to transform overthinking into deeper awareness

Master Your Mind is for the thinkers, the feelers, the quiet warriors battling with their minds in silence. It is your invitation to breathe, reflect, and move forward—with calm and purpose.

By the end of this book, you won't just understand your overthinking - you'll know how to master it.

You'll walk away with clarity, tools, and a new relationship with your mind - one rooted in awareness, stillness, and strength.

TABLE OF CONTENTS

Introduction

"Overthinking is like sitting in a rocking chair. It gives you something to do but it doesn't get you anywhere"

- Glenn Turner

Overthinking is a silent thief of joy. It is a loop of thoughts which keeps blowing in mind continuously. It sneaks into our minds, masquerading as analysis introspection, yet it leaves us feeling paralyzed, overwhelmed and disconnected. How often have you found yourself replaying a conversation in your mind, dissecting every word, or imagining worst case scenarios about the future? Overthinking promises clarity but delivers

, trapping us in a mental maze with no exit confusion.

In a world that celebrates critical thinking and problem solving, overthinking can feel like a natural extension of success. But there is a critical difference: while thinking leads to action and growth, overthinking loops endlessly

This habit isn't just a mental quirk – it's a complex response to uncertainty, fear and the pressure to control outcomes. Whether triggered by past experiences, perfectionism, or the fear of failure, overthinking can affect every aspect of life such as relationships, careers, mental health, self – esteem etc.

But here it is the good thing that overthinking is not a life sentence. By understanding its roots and learning the tools to break free, we can reclaim our mental energy, make better decisions, and live more fully in the present.

This book is not about silencing your mind or abandoning thoughtfulness. It's about finding balance, learning when to trust your intuition, when to dive deep, and when to let go. Together we'll explore why overthinking happens, its impact on our lives, and practical strategies to overcome it.

Welcome to a journey of self- awareness, transformation, and the peace that comes from quieting the mental noise.

The Power of the Mind

"As your thoughts, so your mind. Sow good thoughts, power your mind."

- Swami Srikantananda

First of all necessity to know our mind. Let's understand the basic function of human mind and its power. Several times we intend to do many things- make resolutions to cultivate good habits, to kick certain bad habits, to study with concentration, to do something with concentrated mind. Very often our mind rebels, forcing us to beat a retreat from our efforts at implementing our resolutions. A book is open before us, and our eyes are open. But the mind has started wandering, thinking about some past events or some future plans. Now this is that condition where we are not able to control our mind process and unknowingly we are trapped in the loop of overthinking.

According to the Bhagavad Gita, the undisciplined mind acts as our enemy, whereas a trained mind acts as our friend. So we need to have a clear idea of the mechanism of our mind. Can we train it to obey us, to co-operate us? How can it contribute to transform from overthinking into growth?

The human mind has unique power. This can be illustrated by an example: suppose I meet a person whom I had met somewhere, say about ten years before. I try to recollect when and where I met him and who is he. From the inner recesses of my mind there begins a process of Suddenly I am able to recognize the person as so and so and finally say 'he is the same person I met in such and such a place,' etc. Now I have a firm knowledge about the person.

Analysing the above example, we are able to discern four function of the mind:

Memory: The store house of a memory and impressions our past experiences, presents various possibilities before the mind. This store house is called subconscious mind. It is in this store house that the impressions of our thoughts and actions – good and bad- are stored. The sum total of these impressions determines our thoughts. Our subconscious mind is a very powerful. We can train it to obey us by practising meditation and yoga.

Deliberation and Conceptualization: Not yet sure, the mind examines the many options presented before it. It deliberates several things. This faculty of the mind is called imagination. Imagination and formation of the concepts are also functions of this part of the mind.

Determination and Decision–Making: Brain is the faculty responsible for decision- making. It has the capacity to judge the each and every thing and find what is more desirable. It is also the discriminatively faculty in a person, which enables him or her to discriminate between the real and unreal, between what is to be done and what is to be avoided, what is morally right and what is wrong. It is also the seat of will power so essential for the growth and hence this aspect of the mind concerns us the most.

Consciousness: Appropriating to one self all physical and mental activities such as I see, I hear, I think, I am confused whatever so is called consciousness. As long as the undisciplined body-mind complex, human life is dedicated by events and circumstances of the world; we become happy with pleasurable events, and miserable with adverse circumstances. More the mind gets refined and disciplined; more does one get to know the real condition of thoughts which is a real source of consciousness. Correspondingly, a person becomes more balanced and equipoised in his daily life. Such a person is no longer swayed by any event or circumstances of life and that's why he can understand the thought of overthinking.

What Overthinking Really Means

"If you spend more time to think too much, you will never get it done."

- Bruce Lee

Overthinking is the process of thinking too much, too deeply, or for too long about a particular issue, matter or problem, often in a way that is unproductive.

It involves excessive analysis, worry, anxiety, stress or rumination, where thoughts loop endlessly without leading to clarity or resolution.

The Core Meaning of Overthinking: At its root, overthinking is the mind's attempt to seek certainty, avoids mistakes, or protect us from pain.

However, instead of providing clarity, it often leads to mental exhaustion and inaction. It's not just thinking a lot but it's thinking in a way that traps us rather than frees us.

Key Aspects of Overthinking

- Repetitive Thought Cycle – Thoughts go in circles rather than progressing towards solutions.

- Paralysis by Analysis – The fear of making the wrong the decision leads to indecision.

- Emotional Overload – Excessive thinking amplifies stress, anxiety or self – doubt.

- Illusion of Control – Belief that thinking more will eliminate uncertainty, but it often does the opposite.

The Journey of This Book

"The journey from confusion to clarity begins the moment when you stop treating every thought as the truth."

- Arvind Kaiwartya

What can do this book for you?

Dear readers of course this book will help you to grow faster and you'll see the remarkable changes from tangled mind set to clarity and confidence. This book is not about silencing your thoughts but about setting them free. It's a journey from overthinking to understanding, from hesitation to action, and from self – doubt to clarity. The answers you seek aren't buried in endless analysis – they are waiting in the space beyond it.

In the chapters ahead, we will first understand why overthinking happens, before moving on to practical solutions that help quiet the mental noise. Finally, we'll explore how to transform overthinking into a tool for insight and growth, rather than a roadblock.

This is not just a book to read but it's an experience to engage with. By the end, you won't just understand overthinking; you'll have the tools to break free from it. The journey starts now.

PART ONE: UNDERSTANDING OVERTHINKING

A Resilient Mind

A resilient mind is not one that breaks,

But one that bends,

Learning to grow stronger in the face of every storm.

It is the art of yielding without surrender,

Of standing tall even while bending low,

Of finding strength not resistance,

But in the quiet willingness to grow.

This book is an invitation –

To walk the winding paths of your thoughts,

To meet the shadows without fear,

To listen gently to the restless mind,

And to discover the stillness beneath.

As you begin the journey,

May you remember?

You do not need to silence every thought

To find the peace.

You only need to hold them softly,

And let them pass like clouds across a faithful sky.

For within you is a mind that bends,

And in bending, becomes unbreakable.

- Arvind Kaiwartya

Chapter 1

What Is Overthinking

(A story of the mind's Maze)

The Night Of a Thousand Thoughts: Once there was a boy lived in a small village named Aarav. He was lying down on the bed, staring at the ceiling. The room was dark, but his mind was lit up like a city at midnight – buzzing, restless, and never sleeping. He turned to his side and then to other. The thoughts wouldn't stop.

"Did I say the wrong thing at work place today?"

"Why did she pause before replying to my text?"

"What if I fail this project?"

"I should have handled that situation differently....."

His mind was like a tangled ball of yarn- one thought pulling another, looping endlessly. No matter how much he tried to silence it, but his brain had other plans.

Aarav had always been a thinker. He believed analysing thins made him prepared. But somewhere along the way, his thoughts had stopped being helpful. They weren't guiding him; they were trapping him.

That night, as sleep slipped further away, he whispered to himself, "Why do I do this?"

"Why can't I just stop overthinking?"

The Spiral of Overthinking:

Aarav struggle is something most of us have experienced. We replay our past conversation, worry about future possibilities, and dissect every little detail of our actions. It's like our mind is trying to solve an unsolvable puzzle.

Overthinking isn't just deep thinking. Deep thinking is intentional – it leads to insight.

Overthinking, on the other hand, is a cycle. It's when thinking stops being productive and turns into a mental hamster wheel, spinning but going nowhere.

It comes in different forms:

- Reliving past mistakes, regretting decisions, and feeling trapped in "what – ifs" it's called Rumination.

- Imagining negative scenarios, fearing the worst, and preparing for the things that may never happen is a condition of worrying.

- Over examining options until no decision feels right is the condition of analysis paralysis.

But here is the paradox - overthinking feels like we're in control. We believe if we just think hard enough, we'll find certainty. But in reality, the more we think, the more certain we feel.

The Hidden Cost Of Overthinking

Over time, Aarav's overthinking began to take a toll.

- He began to feel exhausted, even when he hadn't done anything physically demanding.

- Decisions became very harder – secondly he guessed himself so much that he avoided making choices at all.

- He struggled to enjoy the present moment, because his mind as either stuck in the past or racing toward the future.

What Aarav didn't realize was that overthinking wasn't just wasting time – it was draining his confidence. Every overanalysed decision chipped away at his self- trust.

This is the hidden danger of overthinking. It convinces us we're being careful when, in reality we're just standing still.

Breaking the Cycle:

That sleepless night, Aarav finally sat up in bed and asked himself, "What if I just let go?"

For the first time, he tried something new. Instead of wrestling with his thought he simply observed them. He let them pass like clouds drifting in the sky, without chasing or controlling them.

And in that moment, a strange thing happened. His mind, which had been roaring like a storm, began to quiet down.

That was the first step.

Overthinking is not about thinking too much – it's about thinking without direction and the key to breaking free isn't to stop thinking altogether but to learn how to think in a way that serves us, rather than controls us.

Reflection Questions:

- Have you ever found yourself overthinking like Aarav?

- How does overthinking affect your daily life?

- What would happen if you learned to trust yourself more?

- What do you think too much which drains you?

- Why do the people stuck in overthinking?

Chapter 2

The Psychology behind Overthinking

"The mind is its own place, and in itself can make a heaven of hell, a hell of heaven."

- John Milton

Overthinking is often linked to rumination dwelling on past events and worry obsessing over future uncertainties.

Several psychological concepts explain why people overthink:

1. Cognitive Distortions

Overthinking often stems from irrational thought patterns known as cognitive distortions, such as:

- Catastrophizing – Assuming the worst will happen.

- All or Nothing Thinking – Seeing things in extremes e.g., "If I fail, I'm a complete failure."

- Mind Reading – Assuming we know what others think about us.

- Overgeneralization – Drawing board negative conclusions from a single event.

2. The Role Of Anxiety And Stress

- Overthinking is common in Generalize Anxiety Disorder (GAD), where the brain is wired to anticipate threats.

- The fight or fight response gets activated unnecessarily, leading to mental paralysis instead of action.

3. Perfectionism And Control

- Many over thinkers believe if they think long enough, they can prevent mistakes.

- Perfectionists tend to overanalyse decisions because they fear imperfection.

4. The Paradox Of Choice

- Too many options create decision paralysis.

- This leads to analysis paralysis, where thinking replaces action.

Neuroscience of Overthinking:

Overthinking is a neurological loop involving several key brain regions and neurotransmitters.

1. **The Prefrontal Cortex (PFC) – The "Thinking" Brain**

- Responsible for rational decision – making and problem solving.

- In over thinkers, the PFC over engages, analysing situations endlessly instead of taking action.

2. **The Amygdala – The "Fear Centre"**

- Over activity in the amygdala heightens emotional responses, making small problems feel huge.

- Overthinking is often linked to amygdala hijacking, where emotions overpower logic.

3. **(DMN) – The Default Mode Network The "Mind – Wandering" Network**

- The DMN is active when we are not focused on tasks.

- Over active DMN leads to excessive self- referential thinking e.g. worrying about the past or future.

4. **Neurotransmitters And Hormones**

- High cortisol (the stress hormone) increases rumination.

- Low serotonin and dopamine make it harder to regulate emotions and shift attention.

To know about the psychology and neuroscience of overthinking let's have a look some example from real world:-

Case Study 1: Leonardo da Vinci – The Genius Who Overthought Everything

(Historical Example):-

Leonardo da Vinci, one of the greatest minds of all time, was known for his insatiable curiosity. However, few people realize that his genius was often paralyzed by overthinking.

Da Vinci had countless unfinished projects – not because he lacked talent, but because he couldn't stop perfecting his ideas. His note books were filled with sketches, theories and inventions that never came to life. He would start painting a masterpiece, only to abandon it for another idea that suddenly seemed more important. His famous painting "The Last Leaf" took years to complete because he agonised over every tiny detail, sometimes staring at the wall for hours, unable to decide on the right brushstroke.

Modern neuroscientists believe that Da Vinci's over active prefrontal cortex made him prone to perfectionism, while his dopamine- driven curiosity constantly pushed him towards new ideas, creating a cycle of overthinking.

Lesson: Overthinking, even in brilliant minds, can lead to procrastination and unfinished dreams.

Learning: When to let go off perfection and take action is key.

Awareness Vs. Overthinking: Thinking is one of the greatest abilities of the human mind. It allows us to analyse, make decisions, and learn from past experiences. But when thinking turns into overthinking, it becomes a trap. Instead of helping us, it delays and exhausts us. There is a key difference between awareness and overthinking. Awareness leads to clarity and action, while overthinking creates stress and paralysis.

What Is Awareness?

Awareness is consciousness, focused thinking with a clear purpose. It helps you:

- Stay present and see things objectively.

- Analyse situations without fear or self-doubt.

- Recognize mental patterns without getting trapped in them.

- Make decisions based on reality not anxiety.

Example:-

You have an important job interview. Awareness – based thinking sounds like:

- "I will research the company, practice my answer, and focus on my strength."

- "Even if I don't get the job, I will learn from this experience."

Outcome: You feel prepared, confident and ready to take action.

What Is Overthinking?

Overthinking is repetitive, unproductive thinking that:

- Focuses too much on past regrets or future fears.

- Replays the same the thoughts without solutions.

- Creates self- doubts and hesitation.

- Leads to mental exhaustion and inaction.

Example:-

You have the same job interview, but overthinking sounds like:

- "What if I say the wrong thing? What if they don't like me?"

- "What if I don't get the job? What will people think?"

Outcome: You feel anxious, unsure and avoid preparing properly.

Why Does Overthinking Paralyze Us?

Prefrontal Cortex Overload – Overanalysing activates the prefrontal cortex (the part of human brain which is responsible for planning and problem – solving). But when it's overactive, it causes decision paralysis instead of clarity.

Negative Bias – Our brain remembers negative events more than positive ones to protect us from danger. This makes over thinkers focus on worst case scenarios.

Dopamine Addiction – Searching for "perfect answer" gives a small dopamine rush which tricks the brain into continuing the thought loop instead of acting.

Result: Overthinking doesn't protect you, it prevents you from making decisions and moving forward.

Chapter 3

The Impact of Overthinking on Your Life

"Your mind is your instruments. Learn to be its master not its slave."

- Remez Sasson

The Man Who Lived in the Future:

Ethan Reynolds had everything on paper – a stable job, a loving family and a promising future. But inside his mind, he lived somewhere else: in a future that hadn't yet happened.

Every decision, every action was accompanied by a relentless cycle of "what if?"

When he woke up in the morning, his mind started before his body did. What if I say something wrong in the meeting today? What if I mess up and my boss thinks I'm incompetent? What if I lose my job? He would rehearse conversations in his head, anticipate problems that hadn't even occurred and draft escape plans for failures that weren't real.

At work, Ethan was praised for his meticulous planning but he knew the truth his mind wasn't planning, it was panicking. His overthinking caused delays in decisions, second – guessing his choices until opportunities slipped away.

A promotion he deserved? Gone – because he overanalysed his worth until he convinced himself he wasn't ready. A new business idea? Shelved – because he spent months worrying about of taking action.

His relationships suffered too. His wife Claire, noticed how distant he had become. Every time she asked him what was wrong, he would respond, "I'm just thinking." But thinking had become his prison. His mind was never in the present with her; it was in an imaginary catastrophe.

Then one night, everything changed. Ethan lay in bed, his mind spiralling again- this time about a mistake he might have made at work. His chest tightened, his breathing grew shallow and his hands trembled. His heart pounded so hard it felt like it would break free from his ribs.

A panic attack.

Neuroscientifically, Ethan's brain was stuck in an overactive fight or fight response. His prefrontal cortex – the part of the brain responsible for rational thinking –was overridden by his amygdala, the brain's fear centre. His body was reacting to a thought as if it were a real, life threatening danger.

That night, staring at the ceiling, gasping breath, Ethan realised something profound: His thoughts were running his life and they were ruining it.

This was the wake - up call he needed. He began researching overthinking, learning about cognitive distortion, mindfulness and neuroplasticity – the brain's ability to rewire itself. He started practicing present moment awareness, reminding himself that thoughts are just thoughts, not reality. Slowly he learned to break the cycle.

Real – World Takeaway

Ethan's story illustrates how overthinking isn't just "thinking too much" – it's a cognitive trap that can hijack the brain's fear response, leading to anxiety, decision paralysis and even physical symptoms like panic attacks. Neuroscientifically, chronic overthinking strengthens neural pathways that associate everyday situations with stress and danger. The good news is that just as the brain can wire itself into overthinking; it can also rewire itself out of it.

Practical Exercise:

1. Name the thought – say, "This is just my brain predicting the worst – case scenario."

2. Shift Focus – Engage your sense. Feel the ground beneath you, take slow breaths, notice the sounds around you.

3. Ask a reality-check question – "Is this thought based on fact or fear?"

4. Take one small action – Instead of obsessing over the perfect decision, make a decision and move forward.

Overthinking affects nearly every aspects of daily life often in ways that go unnoticed until stress and exhaustion take over. While occasional reflection is beneficial, excessive rumination and analysis can be mentally and physically draining. Here are some another, the most significant ways overthinking impacts daily life.

1. Emotional exhaustion:

How it happens? Overthinking often leads to emotional burnout as the brain works in overdrive, analysing every possible outcome. Constant worry creates a sense of being emotionally overwhelmed.

Real – Life Example: A person spends hours replaying conversation, wondering if they said something wrong. This drains their emotional energy, leaving them fatigued for the rest of the day.

Impact:

- Increased stress and anxiety

- Irritability and mood swings

- Difficulty enjoying the present moment

2. Decision Paralysis:

How it happens? Overthinking leads to inaction. Excessive analysis of pros and cons leads to hesitation. Fear of making the wrong choice results in avoiding decisions altogether.

Real – Life Example: Someone is struggling to choose the right place for outing spends hours researching options, reading reviews and gathering information from other sources and worrying about the "perfect place." At the end they either delay the visit or suddenly change the venue for some reasons that is the cause of overthinking.

Impact:

- Reduced productivity

- Missed opportunity

- Increased self-doubt

3. Sleep Disruption:

How it happens? The mind that won't turn off. The brain replays past mistakes or imagines future problems when it should be resting. Worrying about what needs to be done tomorrow creates unnecessary stress.

Real – Life Example: Lying in the bed, someone replays an embarrassing moment from years ago or plans conversations they might never have, leading to insomnia.

Impact:

- Difficulty falling or staying asleep

- Increased fatigue and decreased focus the next day

- Greater emotional instability due to lack of rest

4. Strained Relationships:

How it happens? Overanalysing social interactions such as constantly analysing other people's words or behaviour leads to misinterpretation. Fear of saying the wrong thing creates social anxiety.

Real – Life Example: A person received a short text reply from a friend and immediately assumes they are upset, leading to unnecessary stress and conflict.

Impact:

- Increased social anxiety

- Misunderstandings and unnecessary conflicts

- Emotional distancing from loved ones

5. Decline in Productivity:

How it happens? The endless loop of thoughts leads to procrastination because it feels overwhelming. Instead of acting, a person keeps refining their ideas, delaying action.

Real – Life Example: A student spends so much time researching for an essay that they never actually write it until the last minute, leading to unnecessary stress.

Impact:

- Missed deadlines and decreased efficiency

- Increased feelings of frustration and self-doubt

- Difficulty prioritizing tasks

6. Increased Anxiety and Self-Doubt:

How it happens? The inner critic grows louder when overanalysing mistakes or failures leads to excessive self-criticism.

Focusing on "what if" scenarios fuels anxiety about the future.

Real – Life Example: A job applicant replays an interview in their head, dissecting every word they said, convincing themselves they performed poorly – even if they actually did well.

Impact:

- Decreased self-confidence

- Higher level of stress and anxiety

- Fear of taking risks or trying new things

7. Physical Symptoms: When the mind affects the body

How it happens? Mental stress manifests in physical ways such as headaches, muscle tension or digestive issues.

The body remains in a state of stress, affecting overall well-being.

Real – Life Example: A person experiencing chronic overthinking feels frequent stomach discomfort or tightness in their chest, mistaking it for a physical illness rather than stress.

Impact:

- Chronic stress-related illnesses

- Fatigue and weakened immune system

- Increased risk of anxiety disorders

PART TWO: IDENTIFYING YOUR OVERTHINKING PATTERNS

Chapter 4

Recognizing Your Mental Traps

"Your Mind is a powerful thing. When you filter it with positive thoughts,   your life will start to change."

- Gautam Buddha

The Night That Changed Everything:

Daniel sat alone at a corner table in a dimly lit café, stirring his coffee absent minded. The steam rose in slow swirls, mirroring the thoughts racing through his mind. He had just received a message from his closest friend, Liam saying: "We need to talk."

Two hours had passed but the words still echoed in Daniel's head.

Catastrophizing kicked in immediately.

"Something's wrong. What if I did something to upset him? What if he's cutting me out of his life?"

Daniel replayed their last few conversations. Had he said anything offensive? Was Liam acting distant lately? He scrolled through old texts, searching for signs he might have missed.

Mind Reading took over.

"He's probably annoyed with me. May be he thinks I've been a bad friend."

His chest tightened. Maybe Liam had found new friends and didn't need him anymore.

Then came Overgeneralization.

"This always happens to me. Every friendship I've had eventually fades away."

A sense of failure crept in.

Emotional Reasoning added fuel to the fire.

"I feel like a terrible friend. That must mean I really am one."

He started at his phone, considering texting an apology-even though he had no idea what he had done wrong. But then he hesitated falling into analysis paralysis.

"Should I wait for wait for him to call first? Should I ask him if everything's okay? But what if that makes things worse? Maybe I should just act normal and pretend I never saw the message?"

His thoughts became a tangle mess. Just then, his phone buzzed again. A second message from Liam popped up:

"Hey, I just wanted to catch up. It's been a while! Let's grab dinner soon."

Daniel let out a breath he hadn't realized that he was holding. All that stress, all that overthinking – for nothing. He had convinced himself of a problem that never existed.

That night, as he walked home, Daniel reflected on how often he fell into these mental traps- jumping to conclusions, assuming the worst, believing his feelings were facts.

And for the first time, he wondered: What if I stopped believing everything my anxious mind told me?

1. The Mind's Hidden pitfalls:

Our minds are powerful, but they often work against us by creating mental traps- cognitive distortions that fuel overthinking.

These traps distort reality, making problems seem bigger and decisions harder. They lead to unnecessary stress, self-doubt and emotional exhaustion.

By recognizing these distortions, we can break free from the cycle of overthinking and gain clarity in our thoughts.

The first step to overcoming overthinking is awareness. Just as Daniel realized how his mind tricked him into believing a problem existed when it didn't, we too, must identify when our thoughts are leading us astray.

In this chapter we will learn the most common mental traps, their impact and how to break free from them.

1. **All Or Nothing Thinking(Black and White Thinking):**

- What it looks like: Seeing things in extreme categories- either a complete success or a total failure.

- Example: "If I don't do this perfectly, I've completely failed."

- Impact: Creates unnecessary pressure, anxiety and discourages progress.

How to Break Free:

- Remind yourself that progress, not perfection is a key.

- Look for middle ground – what's one thing you did well?

- Use a 1 to 10 scale instead of all or nothing.

2. **Catastrophizing (Worst- Case Scenario Thinking):**

- What it looks like: Assuming the worst will happen even with little evidence.

- Example: "If I mess up this presentation, I'll lose my job and my life will be ruined.

- Impact: Causes unnecessary stress, avoidance and decision paralysis.

How to Break Free:

- Ask what's the worst, best and most likely outcome?

- Challenge yourself: "Has this ever happened before? How did I handle it?"

- Use grounding techniques like deep breathing to regain perspective.

3. Overgeneralization

- What it looks like: Seeing one bad experience as a pattern that will always repeat.

- Example: "I failed once, so I'll always fail."

- Impact: Lower self-confidence and creates fear of trying again.

How to Break Free:

- Identify counter examples- times when you succeeded.

- Remind yourself: One event does not define me.

- Reframe mistakes as learning opportunities.

4. Mental Filtering (Only Seeing the Negative)

- What it looks like: Focusing only on the negatives and ignoring positives.

- Example: "I got five compliments but one criticism, so I must have done terribly."

- Impact: Create pessimism, low self-esteem and dissatisfaction.

How to Break Free:

- Keep a daily gratitude journal to track positive.

- Consciously list three good things in any situation.

- Remind yourself that one negative doesn't erase the positives.

5. Mind Reading (Assuming What Others Think)

- What it looks like: Believing you know what others are thinking – usually assuming the worst.

- Example: "She didn't text back immediately, so she must be mad at me."

- Impact: Creates social anxiety and miscommunication.

How to Break Free:

- Ask – "Do I have evidence for this?"

- Use clarification instead of assuming – ask questions.

- Remind yourself that people are often busy not angry.

Chapter 5

Triggers and Patterns of Overthinking

"You will never be free until you free yourself from the prison of your own false thoughts."

- Philip Arnold

The Endless Night of what – ifs:

Sophia lies awake, staring at the ceiling. Tomorrow is a big day – she is giving a presentation at work. At first, she's confident. She knows her material. She is prepared.

Then, a single thought sneaks in: What if I forget what to say?

That thought multiplies:

- What if they ask a question I can't answer?

- What if my voice shakes?

- What if they think I'm not smart enough for his role?

Her mind spirals. She replays imaginary failures, revising her slides at 2AM, standing in front of the mirror rehearsing responses to worst-case scenarios. By morning, she's exhausted, unfocused and overwhelmed.

During the presentation, she stumbles – not because she wasn't capable but because her mind drained her before she eve started.

Sophia's experience reflects a classic trigger-pattern cycle of overthinking:

1. **Trigger:** An upcoming event (like a presentation)

2. **Pattern:** A single doubt escalates into a spiral of anxious thoughts.

3. **Consequence:** Mental exhaustion leads to poor performance, reinforcing the fear.

This story shows that the common triggers trap the people in cycles of rumination and analysis paralysis.

The following triggers are:

1. **Psychological and Emotional Triggers:**

-   **The Fear Loop:** Fear of failure, judgement and regret creates a cycle of endless second-guessing.

-   **The Over Dilemma Analyser's:** When intelligence turns into a mental prison-thinking too much but acting too little.

-   **Emotional Echoes:** Past trauma and unresolved emotions resurface, making decisions feel heavier than they are.

- **The Approval Addiction:** Needing validation from others before making a decision, leading to constant self-doubt.

Real – World Takeaway: Fear magnifies uncertainty, making simple decisions feel overwhelming.

Exercise: Write down three recent decisions you've delayed due to fear. Challenge yourself to make a quick, intuitive choice on at least one today.

2. **Cognitive Traps (How the Mind Tricks You):**

- **Perfectionism's Paralysis:** The belief that if something isn't perfect, isn't worth doing.

- **The Endless "What if Spiral":** Constantly imagining worst-case scenarios instead of realistic possibilities.

- **The Information Overload Effect:** Thinking more research equals more clarity-when in reality, it creates more confusion.

- **The "One Right Answer" Myth:** Believing that only one perfect choice exists, making every decision overwhelming.

Case Study: Lisa, an inspiring writer, spends hours rewriting the same paragraph. Her books remains unfinished because she believes every word must be flawless before she moves forward.

Real – World Takeaway: Perfectionism is just overthinking in disguise. It convinces you that progress isn't good enough.

Exercise: Set a goal to complete something imperfectly – whether it's writing, art or a project. Done is better than perfect.

The 'What If' Spiral: Catastrophizing Every Possibility

Case Study: Raj is invited to speak at a conference. Instead of preparing, he gets stuck imagining every possible way he could embarrass himself. He ultimately declines the opportunity out of fear.

Real- World Takeaway: Most worst-case scenarios never happen and even if they do, they are rarely as bad as we imagine.

Exercise: For every 'What if?" scenario you think of write down an equal number of "What if it goes well?" possibilities.

3. **Environmental and Social Triggers:**

- **Toxic Environments:** Workplace, families or social circles that fuel overthinking through negativity and criticism.

- **Digital Overload:** Constant notifications, social media comparison and unlimited choices leading to mental clutter.

- **Indecisive Surroundings:** Being around people who overthink can reinforce your hesitation.

- **The Expectation Trap:** Society's pressure to "have it all figured out" keeps people stuck in self-doubt.

Case Study: Emily, fresh out of college, feels immense pressure to find a good job. She overthinks every career decision, fearing she'll make the wrong choice and ruin her future.

Real – World Takeaway: There is no single ''correct'' life path. Most successful people took multiple detours before finding their calling.

Exercise: Write down one major decision you're struggling with. Then, list at least three ways it could be a learning experience, no matter the outcome.

1. **Subconscious Triggers(Hidden Patterns That Keep You Stuck):**

   - **Unfinished Business:** Unresolved conflicts or past failures that subconsciously influence current decisions.

   - **The Subtle Power of Routine:** Repeating the same daily patterns that reinforce overthinking instead of action.

   - **Identity - Based Overthinking:** The belief that "I am just an over thinker," reinforcing the behaviour instead of breaking it.

Case Study: Mark is a business man. He had a failed business venture years ago. Even today, he hesitates to start something new because of his past mistakes.

Real – World Takeaway: The past doesn't define your future unless you allow it to.

Exercise: Write a letter to your past self, forgiving any mistakes and giving yourself permission to move forward.

Conclusion: Moving from Overthinking to Action

By identifying and addressing these triggers, you can shift from overthinking to clear, confident action. The goal is not to eliminate thinking but to create a balanced mindset where reflection serves you rather than traps you.

Next Steps:

1. Identify your top two overthinking triggers from this chapter.

2. Apply the recommended exercises for a week and observed any changes.

3. Continue to challenge your thoughts and choose action over hesitation.

Patterns of Overthinking:

"The happiness of your life depends upon the quality of your thoughts."

- Marcus Aurelius

Common Patterns are the following:

1. **Rumination:** This involves repeatedly dwelling on negative thoughts and experience or past events often with a focus on negative aspects without actively seeking solutions.

2. **Worry:** Excessively focusing on potential future problems or negative outcomes.

3. **Overanalyse:** Spending excessive time analysing situations, decisions or people often to the point of paralysis.

4. **Catastrophizing:** This pattern involves anticipating the worst possible outcomes or scenarios, even when there is little evidence to support them of a situation.

5. **Mind – Reading:** Assuming you know what others are thinking or feeling.

6. **Doubt and Second- Guessing:** Over thinkers often question their decisions and actions, constantly seeking reassurance or validation.

7. **Fixation on Uncontrollable Factors:** Overthinking can involve focusing on things outside of one's control, leading to feelings of helplessness and anxiety.

8. **Overgeneralizing:** Making broad conclusions based on a single event or experience.

9. **"What If" Thinking:** Constantly questioning potential outcomes and possibilities.

10. **Analysis Paralysis:** This occurs when overthinking leads to an inability to make decisions or take action due to excessive analysis of pros and cons. Being so overwhelm by the need to

analyse that you become unable to make decisions or take action.

Overthinking thrives on hesitation but clarity is built through action. The choice to break free starts now after reading this chapter. It will help you to decide what to do and what not to do with clear focus on your action to recognise the triggers and patterns of overthinking so that you can easily overcome your overthought. In the next chapter we will learn how to use tools and technique

Chapter 6

Tools for Self – Assessment

"The mind is a superb instrument if used rightly. If used wrongly, however it becomes very destructive."

- Eckhart Tolle

Breaking Free From the Overthinking Trap:

Have you ever spent hours debating a decision, only to feel more confused? Or replayed a conversation so many times that you start doubting what really happened?

Overthinking is like quicksand – the more you struggle, the deeper you sink.

But here is the good thing is that you can escape. The problem isn't that you think too much- it's that you haven't learned how to think effectively. This chapter gives you 9 powerful tools to help you understand your overthinking patterns and take back control.

Challenge: As you go through these tools, pick one that you'll commit to for the next 7 days. Small shifts lead to big transformations.

1. The Overthinking Spectrum Test

Where do you stand on the scale of overthinking?

Before we go further, let's assess your level of overthinking.

Example: Meet Angel

Angel, a beautiful young girl 21 year old was a good student. She was good at study but she was always confused and had self-doubt. She spends hours in study and strives to learn more but the result was not satisfactory.

She overanalyses everything and often lies awake at night replaying the day's conversation or any event happened with her. Her mind feels like a browser with 50 tabs open.

When she saw herself, she realized that due to her overthinking she had lost her control of mind along with good people and relation. Even though it was a crucial time for her to choose the career and make the future bright. She was being supported by every means yet she was not ready to accept her overthought. Finally the situation became the worst and later she felt that: "Wow, this isn't just me being thoughtful – it's a real pattern that's affecting my life."

Try this:

Take the test and reflect: Does this number reflect the quality of life you want?

2. The Thought Record Journal (CBT – Based Tool)

David, a university student, bombed a presentation. That night his mind kept whispering:

"I'm terrible at public speaking. Everyone thanks I'm an idiot."

He used this tool:

- Triggers: His presentation didn't go well.

- Thought: "I embarrassed myself. Everyone will remember this forever."

- Emotion: Anxiety, Shame.

- Distortion: All-or-nothing thinking – one bad presentation doesn't define his ability.

- Reframing: "One bad presentation doesn't mean I'm terrible. I learned what to improve for the next time."

David realized that he had been catastrophizing making one event seem like a disaster.

Try this: For the next three days, write down your overthinking moments and challenge your thoughts.

3. The 3W Method: What, Why and What now?

Example: Meet Lisa

Lisa has been overthinking whether to ask her boss for a raise.

- What? "I'm scared to bring this up."

- Why? "I don't want to be seen as demanding."

- What now? "I'll prepare my key points and request a meeting next week."

Lisa's breakthrough? Taking one small action helped her break the cycle of endless thinking.

Try this: Next time you feel stuck, write down these three questions and answer them.

4. The Decision - Making Grid

Example: Meet Jake

Jake has been in a toxic work environment for years but keeps second – guessing whether to quit.

He used this grid:

Pros: Short – Term - Less stress

Long – Term: New career opportunities

Cons: Short – Term - Financial uncertainty

Long – Term: Risk of career instability

Once Jake saw it visually, he realised his fears were short-term but his gains were long-term. He finally made the decision to leave.

Try this: Use this grid for a decision you've been stuck on.

5. The 5-Second Rule

Leena is a very health conscious girl but she has a habit of overthinking. She always thinks everything in a deep which leads to overthink. She wants to start a fitness routine but keeps overthinking: "What if I look silly due to obesity?"

Instead of getting stuck, she uses 5-4-3-2-1 and immediately puts on her workout shoes. The action breaks the mental loop.

Try this: Next time you overthink, count backward and act.

6. The "Is It Mine?" Exercise

Example: Meet Priya

Priya's family always told her that a "good job" means being a doctor or engineer. But she's passionate about writing.

When she did this exercise, she realised:

"This fear isn't really mine – it's inherited."

For the first time, Priya gave herself permission to pursue what truly made her happy.

Try this: Write down a worry and ask yourself. Who planted this in my mind?

7. The Reverse Lens Perspective Shift

Example: Meet Ryan

Ryan constantly criticizes himself for making mistakes at work. He feels like he's never good enough.

Then, he imagined his best friend in the same situation. Would he say, "Wow, you're such a failure?"

No, he would say, "One mistake doesn't define you. You're doing great."

When Ryan started speaking to himself the way he'd speak to friend, he noticed his anxiety easing.

Try this: Next time you overthink, write down what you'd tell a friend in the same situation.

8. The Time – Test Method

Example: Meet Jenna

Jenna spent three days obsessing over a text she sent to a friend. She feared that she had said something wrong.

She asked herself:

- Will this matter in a year? – No

- What about a month? – Probably not.

- A week? – Unlikely.

She let go of the worry and moved on.

Try this: Test this method on a current worry.

9. The Action Vs. Thought Ratio Test

Example: Meet Alan

Alan wanted to start a YouTube channel, but he kept overthinking:

"What if people don't like my content? What if I fail?"

For three months, he spent 90% of his time worrying and only 10% actually working on his videos.

When he flipped his thought – to – action ratio (spending 70% doing and 30% thinking), his channel finally took off.

Try this: Track your thought – to – action ratio this week. Are you thinking more than doing?

Final Reflection

These tools aren't just exercise – they're your roadmap out of overthinking. The more you observe your thoughts, the less control they have over you.

Which tool stood out to you the most?

Commit to using it for the next 7 days and see what shifts in your mind-set.

PART THREE: PRACTICAL SOLUTION TO OVERCOME OVERTHINKING

Chapter 7

Mindfulness Techniques to Control Overthinking

"The mind is like water. When it's turbulent, it's difficult to see. When it's calm, everything becomes clear."

- Prasad Mahes

Opening Reflection

In the age of noise, silence is a superpower.

In the age of distractions, focus is a rebellion.

And in the age of constant thought, peace is a revolution."

We often blame ourselves for overthinking, but much of it is not your fault. The modern world is designated to steal your attention, feed your fears and hijack your time.

You're not broken – you're just overwhelmed. This chapter is about reclaiming your inner stillness with real tools for a noisy world. Let's deep dive into the use of techniques:

<u>**Modern Methods to Quiet the Mind:**</u>

Section 1: Clear the Clutter

1. Dopamine Detox (Digital Minimalism)

The story: Ravi, a graphic designer, noticed that every time he had a break, he reached for Instagram. What started as "just a scroll" turned into 40 minutes of comparison and anxiety?

He found himself thinking, "I'm falling behind in life." He decided to do a Sunday Dopamine Detox.

He turned off his phone for half a day and went for a long walk, read an old book and took a nap.

By evening something strange happened – his mind was quieter. Not silent, but stiller. That was his first step back to clarity.

How to practice:

- Choose one day a week (or even half a day) to unplug.

- Avoid entertainment, endless scrolling or short – form content.

- Replace it with deep rest, walking, journaling, drawing or just doing nothing.

Exercise:

Pick one upcoming Sunday. Block out 4 hours. Plan ahead what you'll do instead of being online? Journal your experience afterward.

Section 2: Structure the Storm

2. "Thought to Clarity" Journaling

The story: Lisha was stuck in a loop – "what if I mess up this presentation? What if they don't like me?" Her therapist suggested structured journaling.

Instead of random thoughts, she answered four questions:

1. What am I overthinking?

2. Why do I feel this way?

3. What is true? What is just fear?

4. What action can I take?

It felt mechanical at first. But slowly, the mess in her head started to shape itself into clarity. By naming the chaos, she reclaimed her voice.

Exercise:

When overwhelmed, open your notebook and answer these 4 prompts. Do it daily for a week, even if your answers repeat. Your mind will start to slow down.

Section 3: Pause the Panic

3.   90- Second Emotion Reset

The story: Mark received a blunt email from his boss and felt an immediately wave of anger and anxiety. He was about to reply with sarcasm but remembered a neuroscience concept: An emotional chemical reaction lasts only 90 seconds unless you feed it with thought.

He set a timer, took deep breaths and watched the emotion pass like a wave. He didn't avoid the feeling – he just didn't let it define his reaction.

How to practice:

- Notice the feeling rising.

- Set a 90 – second timer.

- Breath, name the emotion. Let it rise and fall.

- Don't chase the thought. Just breathe.

Mantras:

"This is just a wave. I don't need to ride it forever."

Section 4: Calm the Chaos of Choice

4. The Regret Test for Decisions

The story: Aisha had two job offers – one stable, one risky but exciting. She was frozen in analysis paralysis. Her coach asked:

"Which one would you regret not taking 5 years from now?"

The answer was clear. She chose the one aligned with her values, not her fears.

How to practice:

Ask yourself:

- What will I regret more, doing it or not doing it?

- In 5 years, will this still matter?

You'll notice fear becomes quieter when regret speaks louder.

Exercise:

Use this test for one decision this week – big or small. Write your answers and see what your deeper self already knows.

Section 5: Tame the Multitasking Mind

5. The One - Task Rule

The story: Nikhil, a software engineer, was juggling email, meetings and code – all at once. He thought he was being productive but he felt exhausted and unsatisfied. He tried the One-Task Rule: do just one thing for 60 minutes.

No tabs, no phone.

To his surprise, he finished work faster and felt calmer. His anxiety wasn't about the work – it was the switching.

How to practice:

- Choose one task.

- Set a 60 – minute timer.

- Put your phone away. Close all unrelated tabs.

- Focus. No multitasking. No guilt. Just presence.

Exercise:

Try this for one work session today. Journal afterward: How was your focus? Your mood?

Section 6: Get Grounded in the Now

6.   5-4-3-2-1 Grounding Exercise

The story: Tina was at a party when social anxiety hit hard. She felt heart race, her thoughts spiral: "Everyone thinks I'm awkward." She went to the washroom and did this:

- 5 things I see (blue tile, plant, mirror.....)

- 4 things I can touch (my dress, the sink.....)

- 3 things I hear

- 2 things I can smell

- 1 thing I can taste

Her breath returned. The spiral slowed. The moment became manageable.

How to practice:

Use this technique anytime you feel anxiety rising. It brings you back to your senses – and to the present.

Section 7: Train the Brain for Better Movies

7. Mental Movie Visualization

The story: Rafael always imagined worst – case scenarios before interviews – freezing, forgetting words, being judged. A mentor asked him to change the script:

"What if you imagined the best outcome instead?"

So Rafael closed his eyes and visualized himself walking in confidently, smiling, answering with ease. He did this every morning for a week- and when the real interview came, he walked in like he had done it a hundred times. Because he had.

How to practice:

- Imagine the best outcome.

- Engage your senses – what do you see, feel, hear?

- Play this movie in your mind daily.

Exercise:

Before your next event or challenge, close your eyes and rehearse success. Even if it feels fake – it's powerful mental training.

Section 8: Time – Limit the Worry

8.   Worry Scheduling

The story: Maya used to worry all the day – about her health, her family, her future. Her mind never rested. Her coach gave her a strange rule: "Worry only at 6:30 PM."

At first, she resisted. But then she started writing down her worries during the day and saving them for that time. By 6:30, most of them felt silly or resolved. Worry, it turned out, wasn't that persistent if not fed constantly.

How to practice:

- Pick a 15-minute worry window daily(e.g. 6:30 PM)

- During that time, write all your fears.

- Outside that time, tell your mind, "We'll worry later."

Exercise:

Try this for one week. You'll be shocked how little your mind wants to worry when it's allowed to worry freely.

Closing Reflection: Reclaiming the Mind

You don't need to eliminate overthinking completely. That's not the goal. The goal is to understand it, work with it and reduce its grip over your choices. Each of these methods gives you one more tool, one more step, toward a clearer, calmer and more confident life.

Your mind is not the enemy. It just needs a better guide – and that guide is you.

Except above all the methods here are some of the best techniques to help overcome overthinking, organised into practical strategies:

1. **Cognitive Techniques**

- **Challenge Negative Thoughts:** When you notice overthinking, ask yourself, "Is this thought helpful or based on facts?" Replace exaggerated fears with more realistic perspectives.

- **Practice Mindfulness:** Stay in the present moment by focusing on your breath or your surroundings. Mindfulness reduces rumination.

- **Limit "What if" Scenarios:** Set boundaries for your mind. If you catch yourself spinning hypothetical situations, redirect your focus to actionable steps.

2. Behavioural Techniques

- **Set Time Limits for Thinking:** Allocate a specific amount of time (e.g. 10 minutes) to think about a problem, then move on to action or distraction.

- **Action-Oriented Thinking:** Replace analysis with action. Ask yourself, "What small step can I take right now?" Taking action builds momentum and clarity.

- **Journal your Thoughts:** Writing down your worries can help you process them. Once they're on paper, it's easier to let go.

3. Emotional Techniques

- **Self – Compassion:** Overthinking often stems from fear of failure or judgement. Practice self – kindness and remind yourself that no one is perfect.

- **Gratitude Practice:** Shift your focus by listing things you're grateful for. Gratitude redirects attention away from overanalysing negative situations.

4. Lifestyle Changes

- **Physical Activity:** Exercise, even a short walk, releases endorphins and reduces mental clutter.

- **Healthy Routines:** Prioritize sleep, nutrition and hydration, as poor physical health exacerbates mental stress.

- **Digital Detox:** Reduce screen time and limit exposure to information overload, which can feed overthinking.

5. Preventive Techniques

- **Practice Decisiveness:** Learn to make decisions quickly by trusting your gut or setting a deadline.

- **Focus on Solutions, Not Problems:** Instead of dwelling on issues, shift your attention to finding practical resolutions.

- **Limit Over commitment:** Avoid taking on too many responsibilities, which can lead to mental overwhelm.

6. Therapeutic Techniques

- **CBT (Cognitive Behavioural Therapy):** Work with therapist to identify and reframe unhelpful thinking patterns.

- **Meditation Practice:** Incorporate guided meditations or breathing exercises to train your mind to remain calm and focused.

- **Seek Support:** Share your thoughts with a trusted friend or mentor to gain perspective.

By practicing these techniques constantly, you'll train your mind to let go off unproductive thought patterns and focus on what truly matters.

Chapter 8

Practical Exercise for Mental Clarity

"Mental clarity is not the absence of thoughts but it is the presence of awareness."

- Unknown

The Meeting That Never Happened

Arjun was known for being sharp. At thirty – seven, he was a senior strategist at a top consulting firm – respected for his intellect, his poise and his ability to "keep it all together."

But no one saw what happened behind closed doors.

They didn't see the sleepless nights spent rehearsing conversations that never happened.

They didn't hear the noise in his head – the mental loops, the endless simulations, the exhausting need to get everything right.

They didn't know that beneath his success, he was quietly unravelling.

He wasn't burnt out. Not in the traditional sense.

He was mentally crowded, Spiritually cluttered, Philosophically lost.

That Tuesday morning, he was scheduled to lead a high – stake pitch.

Instead, he called in sick. He didn't turn on TV

He didn't check his phone.

He just sat in silence – with a notebook, a black pen and an overwhelming ache to find mental space.

He recalled a quote from Marcus Aurelius:

"Nowhere you can go is more peaceful, more free of interruptions – than your soul."

And for the first time in years, Arjun decided to meet with his own mind.

Step 1: The Mental Dump

He started writing. No structure. No goals. Just thoughts:

- "I'm not doing enough."

- "What if I fail them?"

- "Why do I feel like a fraud?"

Deadlines, Doubts, Disappointments.

They poured out of him like static being drained from a wire.

And in that mess, he found something precious: a pause.

Step 2: The 3x3 Filter

He drew three rough columns:

- What's demanding my time?

- What actually deserves my time?

- What's silently draining me?

He filtered every thought through three simple questions:

- Does this align with the man I want to become?

- Is this creating peace or pressure?

- Is this truly mine to carry or just noise I've inherited?

The result stunned him. Most of his mental weight wasn't from reality – it was from his own unchecked overthinking.

Step 3: Grounding in Presence

He stood up, opened his window, and let the morning light fall on his face.

He picked up his worn copy of Meditations and read slowly:

"You have power over your mind – not outside events. Realize this and you will find strength."

He closed the book and closed his eyes.

And for the first time in months, he felt clear.

Not because the world changed but because he did.

Real – Life Reflection

You don't need to escape from your life to find peace. You need a space where your mind can breathe. Clarity isn't a reward for working harder.

It's the result of stopping long enough to see what truly matters. That day, Arjun didn't solve every problem. But he made one powerful decision:

He chose to stop performing and start leading himself. And that was the beginning of everything.

On the basis of the story of Arjun we can understand clearly the condition of the mind. Here is breakdown of practical exercise for mental clarity, drowning from the research result:

Mindfulness and Focus

1. **Mindful Breathing:** Find a quiet space, sit or lie down comfortably and focus your attention on your breath. Inhale deeply through your nose, feel your lungs fill with air and exhale slowly through your mouth. Pay attention to each breath noticing the sensations of each inhale and exhale with rise and fall of your chest or abdomen.

2. **Mindful walking:** Take a slow walk and pay attention to the each step. Feel the sensation of your feet making contact with the ground and notice the movements of your body and the surrounding environment.

3. **Mindful Eating:** Eat slowly, savour each bite and pay attention to the flavours, textures and aroma of your food and try to eat without distractions such as watching TV or using your phone.

4. **Guided Meditation:** Utilised guided meditation apps or recordings to help you focus and relax. Guided meditation boosts your mind and makes mental health very strong and sharp. Meditate at least 20 minutes in a day as your convenience time and in peaceful environment.

5. **Gratitude Journaling:** Take a few minutes each day to write down things you are grateful for. Never forget to show your gratitude towards God for each and every things happening with you. Always be grateful to the God for this life and for the super unique power that is your brain given by the God. Feel it with the heart and show this from your soul.

6. **Mindful Listening:** Practice active listening in your conversations. Always try to be a good listener and you'll gain a lot of knowledge and wisdom. We know it very well about a well said – **"Listening is gold and Speaking is silver."** Focus on what the other person is saying without interrupting or planning your response.

7. **Visualization:** Close your eyes and imagine a peaceful place or a positive outcome to challenging a situation. Engage your senses by visualising colours, sounds and textures in detail.

Nature and Moment

1. **Spent time in nature:** Spend time in the lap of nature. Nature has very unique power to heal anything provided you should know how to feel that power and you'll see the remarkable changes in life with physically and mentally both. Even short periods of time in nature can improve your mental health.

2. **Regular Exercise:** Aim for 30 minutes of moderate – intensity aerobic exercise, such as brisk walking, most days of the week. If is not possible for anyone who can take simple exercise at home properly.

3. **Yoga and Tai Chi:** This mind – body practices can help to reduce stress and promote relaxation. It's rooted in ancient Chinese martial arts but has evolved into a popular health – promoting practice for all ages and fitness levels. It combines physical moment with mental focus and deep breathing, promoting a sense of calm and well-being.

4. **Mindful Exercise:** Pay attention to the moments of your body and the sensations of your muscles during exercise.

Other Tips:

1. **Self – Care:** Prioritize self-care activities like taking a warm bath, using aromatherapy, practicing sleep hygiene and eating healthily.

2. **Sleep Hygiene:** Aim for 7-9 hours of quality sleep per night. Sleeping is a good and powerful tool to heal most of the diseases. 90 % of the diseases heal during the sleeping hours.

3. **Limit Screen Time:** Try to reduce exposure to screens, especially before going to bed, to improve your sleep and focus. At present most of us always use mobile, TV, Laptop, computer or any devices of using screen reduces our sleep and focus. IT's very harmful for mind and body both. So take a deep sleep and boost your mind.

4. **Connect with Others:** Spend time with loved ones and engage in social activities. Staying connected to others creates feeling of belonging and being loved, cared for and valued. Social connections are important to our mental and physical health. Being connected to others helps to protect against serious illness and diseases.

5. **Set Goals and Priorities:** Having a sense of purpose and direction can improve mental clarity and motivation.

6. **Practice Gratitude:** Regularly acknowledge the good things in your life and practice gratitude for each and every things. It improves our thought and mind.

7. **Practice Mindfulness:** Pay attention to the present moment without judgement.

8. **Take Breaks:** Schedule regular breaks throughout the day to take rest and recharge.

Some scientific research, data on Mindfulness and Mind Clarity derived from – Volume 2, Issue 3, December– 2023 PP 49-59 International Journal of Futuristic Innovation in Arts, Humanities and Management (IJFIAHM) ISSN 2583-6196 IJFIAHM 50

Origin of Mindfulness is from Buddhist and Hindu teachings. Mindfulness practice was famous in the west through the American Professor Emeritus of Medicine Jon – Kabat Zinn's work. His work is popularly famous for Mindfulness – Based Stress Reduction. Mindfulness has surged popularity over decades and its applicability has been seen across a wide range of physical illness as well as psychiatric disorders specially anxiety and depression (Ran & Kumar,2018). Scientists have theoretically and empirically linked mindfulness to improve physiological well-being in a variety of domains (Siegel, 2007). Mindfulness as a practice has been explored as a method to promote general health and well-being – e.g. as a preventative technique (Baer, Lykins & Peters, 2012), (Brown & Ryan, 2003), (Jazaieri & Shapiro, 2010), (Lykins & Baer, 2009), (Orzech, Shapiro, Brown & Mckay, 2009), (Shapiro & Jazaieri, 2015)

For Stress reduction and mental clarity meditation is very important for mind wellness. Meditation practice an individual is asked to focus on a single object such as breath, mantra or visual image (Kabat – Zinn), (Baer R.A., 2003). Mindfulness can balance through meditation practices or moments throughout the day. Through meditation keep mind strong and calm. Mindfulness practices extend beyond formal meditation sessions, finding relevance in educational settings, workplaces and personal relationships. The positive outcomes of mindfulness, both for individuals and communities, emphasize its role as holistic approach to well-being.

Key aspects of mindfulness include:

1. **Present Moment Awareness:** Mindfulness encourages individuals to be fully engaged in the present moment, paying attention to their thoughts and experiences as they unfold.

2. **Non – judgemental Observation:** Practitioners of mindfulness aim to observe their thoughts and feelings without attaching judgement. This involves accepting thought and emotions without labelling them as good or bad.

3. **Focused Attention:** Mindfulness often involves directing attention to a specific focal point such as the breath, bodily sensations or an external object. This helps in cultivating concentration and reducing mental distractions.

4. **Acceptance:** Mindfulness involves accepting things as they are in present moment, acknowledging one's thoughts and feelings without trying to change or supress them.

5. **Mindful action:** Beyond formal meditation, mindfulness can be applied to daily activities. This means being fully present and engaged in routine tasks, whether it's eating, walking or interacting with others.

The practice of mindfulness has its roots in various contemplative traditions including Buddhism but it has gained widespread recognition and adaptation in secular contexts including psychology and wellness. Mindfulness – Based intervention, such as Mindfulness – Based Stress Reduction (MBSR) and Mindfulness – Based Cognitive Therapy (MBCT) have been developed to help individuals manage stress, improve mental well-being and enhance overall quality of life. Scientific research suggests that regular mindfulness practice may have a range of benefits, including stress reduction, improved focus and concentration, better emotional regulation and enhanced overall psychological well-being. Stress is a natural response to challenging or threatening situations but chronic or excessive stress can have negative impacts on health and well-being. Stress reduction techniques and strategies are aimed at managing stress levels to prevent its detrimental effects. Key components of stress reduction include:

1. **Relaxation Techniques:** Engaging in activities that promote relaxation, such as deep breathing, meditation, progressive muscle

relaxation and guided imagery can help the nervous system and reduce stress.

2. **Physical Activities:** Regular exercise has been shown to be an effective way to reduce stress. Physical activity releases endorphins which are chemicals in the brain that acts as natural stress relievers.

3. **Time Management:** Efficiently organising and managing time can reduce the feeling of being overwhelmed. Prioritising tasks and breaking them into smaller, more manageable can be helpful.

4. **Healthy Lifestyle choices:** Adequate sleep, a balanced diet and proper hydration contribute to overall well-being and can enhance the body's ability to cope with stress

5. **Social Support:** Maintaining strong social connection and seeking support from friends, family or a support network can provide emotional assistance during stressful time.

6. **Mindfulness and Meditation:** Practices that promote mindfulness such as meditation and mindfulness breathing can help individuals stay focused on the present moment and reduce anxiety associated with future concerns.

7. **Cognitive Behavioural Techniques:** Identify and challenging negative thought patterns can be effective in reducing stress. Cognitive Behavioural Therapy (CBT) is a therapeutic approach that often includes such techniques.

8. **Hobbies and Leisure Activities:** Engaging in activities that bring joy and relaxation such as hobbies or leisure activities can serve as a healthy distraction and contribute to stress reduction.

9. **Setting Realistic Goals:** Establishing achievable and realistic goals helps in preventing the feeling of being overwhelmed. Breaking larger tasks into smaller, more manageable steps can make goals attainable.

10. **Mind-Body Practice:** Practices like yoga and physical movement with mindfulness, promoting relaxation and stress reduction. By incorporating these strategies into one's lifestyle, individuals can effectively manage and reduce stress, leading to improve overall well-being and a better quality of life.

It's important to recognise that stress reduction is a personalised process and individuals may find different techniques more or less effective based on their preference and needs.

Mental Clarity: Mental clarity clearly stated that it is transparent and focused thinking of person without taking over burden of thoughts and its process. Mental clarity gives the right direction to the decision – making process and where the mind is free from various mental issues like confusion, distractions and mental fogginess.

"It involves the ability to concentrate, making decisions and process information with precision and efficiency. When you experience mental clarity, your thoughts are organised and coherent and you can see things more objectively. Key points of mental clarity include:

1. **Clear Thinking:** Thoughts are organised and coherent, making it easier to understand complex ideas and solve problems.

2. **Focused and Concentration:** The ability to concentrate on a task without being easily distracted. Mental clarity allows you to stay focused on the present moment and the task at hand.

3. **Quick Decision Making:** Clarity of mind enables you to make decisions more efficiently and with confidence. You can weigh options, assess consequences, and choose a course of action more easily.

4. **Emotional Stability:** Mental clarity often contributes to emotional stability. When your thoughts are clear, you may find it easier to manage stress, anxiety and other emotion.

5. **Improved Memory:** A clear mind is generally associated with better memory and recall. Information is processed more effectively, making it easier to remember and retrieve.

6. **Enhanced Problem Solving:** Mental clarity allows for a more systematic and effective approach to problem solving. You can analyse situations, identify potential solutions and make informed choices. Several factors can influence mental clarity including:

i) ***Stress Management***: Chronic stress can cloud the mind, making it difficult to think clearly. Effective stress management techniques such as mindfulness and relaxation exercises can contribute to mental clarity.

ii) **Adequate Sleep**: Lack of sleep can impair cognitive function and contribute to mental fogginess. Ensuring sufficient and quality sleep is essential for maintaining mental clarity.

iii) **Mindfulness practices:** Techniques like meditation and mindfulness can help to calm the mind, reduce mental chatter and promote mental clarity.

iv) **Reduced Distractions:** Minimizing external distractions and creating an organised environment can contribute to improved focus and mental clarity.

Cultivating mental clarity is a holistic process that involves addressing both mental and physical aspects of well-being. It's about creating an environment and adopting practices that support clear thinking and effective cognitive function. Mindfulness practices can be effective tools for stress reduction and promoting mental clarity. Above already some mindfulness techniques are described which you can incorporate into your daily routine. Integrating these mindfulness techniques into your routine can contribute to reduce stress and improved mental clarity over time.

By doing all these exercise we can easily reach our ultimate goal that is mental clarity. In the next chapter we'll learn to use the best Cognitive Behavioural Tools to disrupt overthinking.

Chapter 9

Cognitive Behavioural Tools to Disrupt Overthinking

The story: Maya and the Spiral of Self-Doubt

Maya was the kind of person everyone described as "thoughtful." But inside, she was exhausted. Every decision – big or small felt like a trap.

One morning, she received a short message from her friend:

"Hey, can we talk later?"

A simple sentence but in Maya's mind, it became a maze.

Did I do something wrong? Did I say something weird yesterday? Maybe she is upset with me or maybe something happened to her. But what if she wants to end the friendship?

By lunch time, she had already imagined five different scenarios – none of them was good.

It was always like this. At work, she hesitated to share ideas because she feared sounding foolish. After every meeting, she replayed her words, scanning for flaws. Socially, she second-guessed texts before sending them. In relationships, she overanalysed silences and pauses.

One evening, tired of mental noise, Maya searched "How to stop overthinking everything" online. That's when she discovered Cognitive Behavioural Therapy (CBT).

She learned that her mind wasn't broken – it was following a pattern. CBT taught her how thoughts, emotions and behaviours are connected. More importantly, it showed her how to identify distorted thinking patterns and challenge them. She began using techniques like:

- Thought journaling

- Cognitive distortions identification

- Reality Testing

- The STOP technique (Stop, Take a breath, Observe Proceed)

Slowly, Maya began to catch her thoughts before they spiralled. She started asking herself, "What else could be true?"

And for the first time in years, her mind started to feel like a place of clarity not chaos.

Now this is the question for you my dear friends and readers – what is actually make us entangle and how we come to know that issues? Here, the 5 main steps in Cognitive Behaviour Therapy (CBT) involve identifying and challenging negative thought patterns and behaviours, then replacing them with more positive and effective ones.

These steps include:

1) Identifying situation, thoughts or behaviours that may be contributing to a problem.

2) Becoming aware of unproductive thoughts and their impact.

3) Creating alternative more positive replacement thoughts.

4) Practicing these new thoughts and behaviours and

5) Maintaining progress and preventing relapse.

Here's a more detailed breakdown with 10 best techniques of cognitive behavioural tools to disrupt overthinking:

1. Cognitive restructuring (Thought Challenging)

The Tool: Identify irrational or automatic thoughts and replace them with balanced, evidence-based ones.

Case Example - The Presentation Paralysis:

Ravi, a young professional, spirals every time he is scheduled to present. "They'll think I'm incompetent," his mind insists. He sweats, avoids eye contact and sometimes even fakes sick. One day, his therapist asks –

"What is the proof?" Ravi reflects and Realises that he's never once received negative feedback. His fear is not fact.

Practical Exercise:

- Write down your fearful thought.

- Ask: i) Is this 100% true?

    ii) What's the evidence for and against it?

    iii) What would I tell a friend who thought this?

- Replace it with a balanced thought.

Reflection Takeaway:

Most overthinking is not a mirror of reality but a mirror of fear.

2. Behavioural Experiments

The Tool: Test your thoughts with small actions instead of mental rehearsal.

Case Example – The Invisible Student

Anjali, a college student believes if she speaks in the class, others will roll their eyes. Her therapist challenges her to raise her hand once during the week. She hesitantly does and to her surprise, her peers nod in agreement. The thought crumbles.

Practical Exercise:

- Identify one fearful prediction.

- Design a mini experiment to test it.

- Reflect: What actually happened? Was it as bad as you imagined?

Reflection Takeaway:

You can't fight false beliefs with logic alone – sometimes, you need action.

3. Thought Records (Daily Thought Logs)

The Tool: Track, analyse and reframe persistent thoughts.

Case Example – The Late Reply Spiral:

Tariq overthinks every message. If a friend replies late, he assumes he's done something wrong. Through daily thought logs, he notices this pattern and starts identifying the distortion: mind reading. By journaling daily, he begins to challenge this loop.

Practical Exercise:

Use a table like this:

Situation > Emotion > Automatic Thought > Cognitive Distortion > Alternate Thought > Outcome

Reflection Takeaway:

Writing down your mind's patterns turns the vague fog of thought into something you can navigate.

4. Cognitive De-fusion

The Tool: Separate yourself from your thoughts – don't fuse with them.

Case Example – The "I am not good enough" Tape:

Megha, a perfectionist hears the same voice daily. "You're not doing enough." Her therapist suggests that she should say this phrase in a cartoon voice. It loses its emotional grip.

Practical Exercise:

- Pick a recurring negative thought.

- Say it out loud in a silly voice or sing it.

- Watch how the weight of the thought shifts.

Reflection Takeaway:

Your thoughts are not truths. They're just mental weather.

5. The 3 – Column Technique

The Tool: Break down thoughts into rational and irrational components.

Case Example – Social Overthinking:

Jason didn't get a reply after a date and assumed: "She hated me." After using the

3-column technique, he sees the irrational leap.

Exercise Format:

Situation   Automatic Thought   Rational Response

Reflection Takeaway:

Distorted thoughts shrink when they're placed side by side with reason.

6. Socratic Questioning

The Tool: Ask thoughtful questions to undermine cognitive distortions.

Case Example – Career Catastrophe:

Sana thinks missing one promotion means she'll fail in life. Her coach asks her through these:

- What's the evidence for that?

- What's a more likely outcome?

- What have I survived before?

Practical Exercise:

Next time you spiral, ask

- "Is this fear based on past or present evidence?"

- "If this happened to a friend, what would I say?"

Reflection Takeaway:

Overthinking collapses when examined with calm curiosity.

7. Worry Time Technique

The Tool: Schedule your worries instead of letting them hijack your day.

Case Example – The Midnight Thinker:

Arvind used to stay up analysing every detail of his day. Now, he gives himself 15 minutes at 10:30 before going to the bed to worry and journals during that time only. Surprisingly many thoughts feel irrelevant by the time the window arrives.

Practical Exercise:

- Pick a "worry window" (10 – 15 min).

- When a thought arises, jot it down and tell yourself, "I'll think about it during worry time."

- Revisit only if needed.

Reflection Takeaway:

Worries grow in chaos – but shrink when you put them on a leash.

8. Decatastrophizing

The Tool: Scale down the imagined apocalypse in your head.

Case Example – The Public Blunder:

Nina fears forgetting her lines in a play. Her coach guides her:

- What's the worst that could happen?

- What's likely?

- Could you handle it?

She realises: forgetting a line isn't career ending.

Practical Exercise:

Write down these points:

- Worst-case scenario

- Best-case scenario

- Most likely scenario

Then ask – "Can I cope with the worst?"

Reflection Takeaway:

Clarity returns when you shrink the monster in your mind.

9. Core Belief Work

The Tool: Target deep – rooted beliefs that fuel repetitive overthinking.

Case Example – "I must be perfect to be loved."

Amit's overthinking stems from an old core belief that failure means rejection. Through guided journaling and affirmations, he begins healing this narrative.

Practical Exercise:

- Ask: "What belief keeps showing up behind my thoughts?"

- Challenge it gently.

- Write a new belief: "Even when I fail, I am worthy."

Reflection Takeaway:

To quiet your thoughts, you must sometimes heal your wounds.

STOP Technique

10. Tool: A rapid – response tool to disrupt spirals in real time.

Steps:

- S – Stop

- T – Take a breath

- O – Observe your thought and feeling

- P – Proceed mindfully

Case Example - The Text Over analyser:

Mahi rereads texts obsessively. Now, she uses STOP the moment, she catches herself.

One breath. One pause. One mindful choice.

Exercise:

Next time you catch yourself spiralling, pause and go through STOP.

Bonus: Set this as your phone wallpaper as a reminder.

Reflection Takeaway:

You don't always need to fix the thought. You just need to pause it.

Other Powerful Techniques:

1. **The 3C's Technique:** The 3C's in cognitive psychology, specifically in the context of cognitive restructuring within Cognitive Behavioural Therapy refers to the steps of – Catching, Checking and Changing unhelpful or inaccurate thoughts. This technique is a mnemonic device to help individuals identify and

challenging negative thought patterns and replace them with more balanced and helpful ones.

The Key Takeaways:

Awareness + Reality Check + Reframing = Freedom from thought spirals.

2.   **The 4D's Technique:** In psychology the "4Ds" are a set of criteria used to help determine if a behaviour or thought pattern is considered abnormal and indicative of a psychological disorder. These are – Deviance, Dysfunction, Distress and Danger.

Elaboration:

Deviance: This refers to behaviours, thoughts or emotions that significantly deviate from what is considered typical or statically normal within a particular culture or society. It's about how far a behaviour is from the "norm."

Dysfunction: This describes behaviours or thoughts that hinder a person's ability to function effectively in their daily life, work or relationships. It's about the impact of the behaviour on a person's ability to cope with everyday situations.

Distress: This refers to the experience of emotional pain or suffering associated with the behaviour or thought pattern. It's about the subjective feeling of discomfort or unhappiness.

Danger: This describes behaviours that pose a risk to oneself or others, such as

self-harm or violent behaviour. It's about the potential for harm to be caused by the behaviour.

These four criteria are often used in combination when evaluating whether a person's behaviour warrants a psychological diagnosis. It's important to note that these criteria are not absolute and can be complex to interpret, as they often exist on a spectrum rather than being clearly defined as either abnormal or normal. Additionally, the relative importance of each "D" can vary depending on the specific disorder being considered.

The Key Takeaways: Disrupt the cycle by managing emotions, questioning thoughts and choosing clarity over paralysis.

All these powerful techniques are very important to come out from the entangled mind where the continuous thoughts are running in the head. All the tools and practical exercises will help you to understand the real condition of the mind that every time what we think is right or harmful for us. There are so many life examples and practical are described which can be done very easily to know about our thought due to that we always being in dilemma. By using all these techniques one can easy disrupt the overthinking and can control the negative thoughts.

Summary: Cognitive Behavioural Therapy (CBT) gives us powerful, practical tools to break free from the trap of overthinking. It helps us spot the patterns in our thoughts that keep us stuck – like jumping to conclusions, expecting the worst or seeing things as all or nothing. Once we recognize these unhelpful thinking styles, we can start to challenge them and see things more clearly.

Some key CBT tools include thought records (writing down your worries and analysing them), cognitive restructuring (learning to question and reframe negative thoughts), behavioural experiments (testing your fears in real life) and worry scheduling (giving your worries a time and place so they don't take over your day).

By using these techniques, we move from overthinking to action, from confusion to clarity. CBT doesn't just stop overthinking – it helps us build healthier, more balanced ways of thinking that lead to peace of mind.

Journaling Prompts with Example answers:

1. Write about three common thought patterns or distortions you have noticed in your overthinking. How do they usually show up?

    Example answer: "I often assume the worst will happen (catastrophizing), I think people are judging me (mind – reading), and I see things as either a success or failure (all- or- nothing thinking). These usually show up when I'm nervous about work or social situations.

2. Think of a recent negative thought you had. If you could reframe it differently, what would the new perspective be?

   Example answer: "I thought, I'm terrible at public speaking. Reframed, it could be: I'm still learning and every time I speak, I get a little better."

3. Describe a time when overthinking held you back. What small action could you have taken to test your assumptions?

   Example answer: "I spent hours worrying about sending an email because I thought it wasn't good enough. I could have just sent it earlier and asked for feedback instead of trying to make it perfect."

4. Imagine setting a daily "worry time." How do you think it would change your mental and emotional space during the rest of the day?

Example answer: "I think it would help me feel less overwhelmed. If I knew I had time later to think about my worries, I could focus more on what I'm doing without feeling distracted.

5. Of all CBT tools mentioned, which one feels most useful or approachable for you right now? Why?

   Example answer: "worry scheduling feels the easiest to try because it doesn't require a lot of steps – I can just set aside 15 minutes and write down my worries at that time.

"Each thought you challenge, each belief you transform, is like clearing the fog on a quiet mirror – revealing the calm, steady reflection of your truest mind beneath the noise."

In the next chapter we will elaborate how to transform overthinking into clarity and will see many life's inspiring example.

PART FOUR: TRANSFORMING OVERTHINKNG INTO CLARITY

Chapter 10

Developing a Resilient Mind Set

"Do not judge me by my success, judge me by how many times I fell down and got up back again."

- Nelson Mandela

A resilient mind set, both psychologically and neuroscientifically, is characterised by the ability to adapt well in the face adversity, trauma and significant sources of stress. Psychologically, it involves strong coping mechanisms, a positive outlook and the ability to learn and grow from challenging experiences. Neuroscientifically, it's linked to specific brain regions and neural pathways that regulate emotional responses, mood and decision-making.

The Power of a Resilient Mind set

The Story: The Man Who Rebuilt the Bridge

There was once a civil engineer named Ayaan who had built one of the most important bridge in a remote Himalayan village. The bridge was more than a structure to him – it was a symbol of everything he had survived: childhood poverty, academic rejection and the grief of losing both the parents at young age. When the bridge was completed, it connected lives, gave children access to schools, and brought families together.

Three years later, a rare but catastrophic flood destroyed the bridge.

When Ayaan arrived to see the remains, his heart collapsed. Villagers stood around helplessly, whispering, "He is not going to come back after this." One even said, "No one can handle losing everything twice."

But Ayaan didn't leave. He sat on a stone for hours, watching the water flow. Then he did something strange – he picked up a single piece of debris and began carving markings into it. A child came and asked, "What are you doing?"

Ayaan replied, "I'm designing the second version of the bridge, but a better one, using insights from the flood. More stable, Wider and Stronger.

Villagers now called him "the man who listens to disasters."

Psychological insight:

Ayaan's story embodies the core of resilience not avoiding pain, but transforming pain into purpose. Psychologically, resilience is not a fixed trait but a set of learned cognitive and emotional skills. A resilient mind learns from hardship, engages in cognitive reframing (seeing the event as an opportunity for growth), and uses emotional regulation to respond instead of react.

Neuroscience shows that resilient individuals have higher prefrontal cortex activity, allowing better regulation of the amygdala (Which triggers fear and emotional reactivity).

Ayaan's pause on the stone wasn't passive – it was active emotional integration, allowing space between experience and reaction.

Practical Exercise: Resilience Reframe Journal

- Recall a recent setback that hurt you deeply. Write it down in detail.

- Ask: What did this event teach me about myself, life or others?

- Write three reframed statements that begin with:

i) "Because of this, I've learned..."

ii) "This pain has opened a doorway to..."

iii) "If this hadn't happened, I wouldn't have discovered..."

Do this weekly with any challenge you face. Over the time, your brain starts scanning for meaning and growth instead of just threat and failure.

Reflection Takeaways:

Resilience is not a denial of pain. It's the inner strength to walk into the storm and come out wiser. Like Ayaan, your pain can be your blueprint– if you allow your mind to build, not break.

Resilience Is a Daily Practice, Not a Personality Trait

We often believe that some people are born resilient, like they possess a secret strength the rest of us don't. But the truth is? Resilience is not inherited. It is trained. It's a set of thoughts, behaviours and choices we make daily.

In psychology, resilience is defined as the process of adapting well in the face of adversity, trauma, tragedy, threats or significant sources of stress. It doesn't mean avoiding distress. It means navigating it with a mindset that asks: what now? Instead of Why me?

Research in positive psychology by Dr. Martin Seligman shows that resilience is most strongly tied to three core beliefs:

1. I can influence what happens next (Internal focus of control)

2. My struggles have meaning (Purpose)

3. This moment is not permanent (Temporal framing)

A resilient mind-set is like a mental muscle – it strengthens with conscious use and like physical training, it grows stronger not despite discomfort but because of it.

Real – Life Example:

The Silent Comeback of a Burnt – Out Doctor

Dr. Tara Menon was a rising medical star in Mumbai. She is known for her razor – sharp diagnostic skills, she went to physician in her department. But inside, she was quietly breaking. Working 16 hours shifts, skipping meals and shouldering the emotional burden of patients' lives, Tara hit a wall.

One evening, she collapsed during a shift. Diagnosis: extreme burnout, adrenal fatigue and depression.

Her first instinct? Shame. "I'm supposed to save people. Now I need saving?"

But over the next six months, Tara did something remarkable. She stopped. She sought therapy. She read books on burnout and neurobiology. She meditated. She walked every morning without checking her phone. Slowly, she returned to work – not as the saviour but as a human being.

Today, she runs workshops for medical interns on emotional resilience. She teaches them that "your strength is not in pushing harder, but in pausing wiser."

The Four Pillars of Resilience

Let's explore what Dr. Tara and Ayaan had in common. Research and real – life practice reveal that resilient people consistently engage in four key behaviours:

1. **Emotional Awareness** – They allow themselves to feel. Instead of supressing pain, they process it.

2. **Cognitive Reframing** – They don't get stuck in "Why me?" Instead, they shift perspective to "What now?" or "What can this teach me?"

3. **Purpose Orientation** – They link their suffering to something bigger – a mission, a meaning, a lesson.

4. **Flexible Thinking** – They adapt when plan A fails, they don't crumble – they reorganize for plan B, C, or even Z.

Practical Exercise: Your Mental Resilience Map

Draw a circle in the middle of a page and write "Challenge" inside it.

Then draw four lines outward, each labelled:

- How I feel about this

- What I'm learning from this

- What this could mean later

- How I can respond instead of react

Spend 10 minutes writing under each point. This builds emotional literacy meaning making and response flexibility – three corner stones of resilience.

Repeat this every time you're faced with a challenge. You're not just solving a problem but you're rewiring your mind set to face future storms with greater clarity.

Closing Thought: Becoming the Bridge

Remember Ayaan, who rebuilt the bridge?

What he really rebuilt was himself. Every plank, every nail, every design tweak was a reflection of his new internal architecture. He became a stronger bridge between the past and future, not just for his village, but for himself. So too you can.

You are not the storm. You are the builder. You are the unbreakable thread.

Final Reflection Question:

"What has life been trying to teach me through my hardest moments?"

Take a few quiet minutes with this question. Don't rush to answer it. Let the question echo inside. Sometimes, resilience isn't about having the answer – it is about becoming someone who can carry the question with grace.

Mindfulness Prompt: The Resilience Breath

This practice helps ground you in the present while connecting you to your inner strength.

1. Sit comfortably. Close your eyes.

2. Inhale slowly for 4 counts, imagining you are breathing in calm, stability and trust.

3. Hold for 2 counts, acknowledging your inner stillness.

4. Exhale for 6 counts, releasing tension, fear and helplessness.

5. Repeat for 5 rounds.

As you breathe, silently repeat:

"I am not what happened to me. I am who I choose to become."

Let this breath carry you forward. Let it be your quiet power.

"Some storms come to break you. Others come to show you that you were the shelter all along."

Absolutely this final line tells us to the inner strength, transformation and becoming a source of stability even in chaos.

Further we will explore the different aspects of Resilience Mindset that is Psychological Resilience and Neuroscientific Resilience.

Psychological Resilience:

1) **Coping Mechanisms:** Resilient individuals utilize effective strategies to manage stress, such as problem-solving, emotional regulation, and seeking social support.

2) **Positive Outlook:** They tend to maintain a positive perspective, even in the face of setbacks and are more likely to find meaning in difficult situations.

3) **Learning and Growth:** They view challenges as opportunities for personal growth and development, rather than as insurmountable obstacles.

4) **Self-Efficacy and Optimisms:** Resilient individuals possess a strong sense of self-efficacy, believing in their ability to cope with challenges and are more optimistic about the future.

5) **Emotional Intelligence:** They are able to recognize and regulate their emotions effectively, which helps them navigate difficult situations with greater ease.

Neuroscientific Resilience:

1) **Left Prefrontal Cortex:** Resilient brains demonstrate higher activity in the left prefrontal cortex, a region associated with emotional regulation, mood and meaning – making.

2) **Connectivity with the Amygdala:** Resilient individuals exhibit stronger connectivity between the left prefrontal (the brain's "fear centre"), allowing for faster recovery from stressful experiences.

3) **Neuroplasticity:** The brain's ability to adapt and change in response to experiences is crucial for resilience. Resilient individuals show a greater capacity for neuroplasticity, enabling them to recover from stress and trauma more effectively.

4) **Hormonal Regulation:** Resilient brains may exhibit better regulation of stress hormones like cortisol, preventing prolonged stress responses and associated negative effects.

5) **Neurotransmitters:** Neurotransmitters like dopamine and serotonin play a role in mood, motivation and reward, and their levels may be more stable in resilient individuals.

In essence, a resilient mindset is a combination of psychological strength and neurobiological processes that allow individuals to not only survive adversity but also to thrive in its aftermath.

Reflection Question: What is the 7 C's to build resilience?

Resilience: The 7 C's of resilience is a model developed by paediatrician Dr. Kenneth Ginsburg to help young people (and really, anyone) inner strength and coping skills. To cultivate resilience in your life, it's important to apply the principles of 7 Cs:

1. **Competence** – Knowing you have the skills and strengths to handle challenges.

2. **Confidence** – A strong belief in your own abilities, built by recognizing your achievement.

3. **Connection** – Having close ties to family, friends, community – relationship that offers support.

4. **Character** – Developing a strong sense of right and wrong, and living with integrity.

5. **Contribution** – Realizing that making a difference to others adds meaning to your life.

6. **Coping** – Having healthy strategies to deal with stress and hardship (like mindfulness, exercise, and seeking help).

7. **Control** – Understanding that you can influence outcomes through your decisions and actions.

Each "C" builds on the others – together they create a strong foundation for resilience, especially when facing life's inevitable ups and downs.

Quick Tips: You don't have to master all 7 C's at once. Even strengthening one or two can create momentum in the others.

The Key Takeaway:

Resilience is not about ever falling – it's about learning to rise with greater clarity and strength each time.

A resilient mindset transforms overthinking into insight, fear into growth, and uncertainty into opportunity.

By shifting from reactive thinking to reflective awareness, you cultivate the ability to face challenges with composure, adapt with purpose, and choose responses aligned with your highest self.

Chapter Summary: This chapter explores the transformative power of resilience – the inner ability to not only endure adversity, but to grow through it. It opens with the moving story of Ayaan, an engineer who rebuilds a bridge after a devastating flood, symbolizing the human capacity to rebuild after internal collapse.

The chapter then unpacks the psychological foundation of resilience, drawing from positive psychology and neuroscience. It emphasizes that resilience is not a fixed trait but a trainable mind-set built on:

- Emotional awareness

- Cognitive reframing

- Purpose orientation

- Flexible thinking

A real life case study of Dr. Tara Menon, a doctor recovering from burnout, illustrates how resilience is practiced in the everyday trenches of modern life – not in grand gestures but in small, consistent acts of healing and reflection.

Practical exercises like the Resilience Reframe Journal and Mental Resilience Map provide readers with concrete tools to build mental toughness and clarity.

The chapter ends with a calming Resilience Breath mindfulness prompt and a reflective question to deepen personal insight.

Through powerful stories and grounded psychology, readers are reminded that they are not defined by what breaks them – but by how they choose to rebuild.

Chapter 11

Building New Thought Habits

"Each thought is a seed.

Every habit is a season.

What you plant today becomes the life

You harvest tomorrow."

- James Allen

How to Plant, Nurture and Transform the Mind You Live Within.

"Your mind is not fixed, nor is your thoughts final.

Every belief you hold, every idea you carry, every habit you nurture – they are all living, growing things.

In the same way a gardener shapes the beauty of a landscape, you have the power to shape the nature of your own mind.

Thought by thought, habit by habit, you are always creating yourself a new."

In this chapter, we will explore how to plant and nurture the kinds of thoughts that create clarity, resilience and inner peace.

You will see through stories how different approaches – structured and flowing – can both lead to mental strength and transformation.

You'll also be invited to choose your own method for tending your mental garden, so that new thought habits can naturally bloom in your life.

Let us begin – in the gardens of the mind.

Where Thoughts Take Root

Every mind is a garden, unseen yet always alive.

Some gardens are crafted through careful design, others through the quiet rhythm of trust.

Whether you build with steady hands or sing your seeds into bloom, the arts remains the same:

You shape your world by the thoughts you choose to nurture.

Here are two journeys, two ways of growing – May you find yourself in one or both.

Journey One: Elias – The Engineer of His Mind

Elias was a man of deep thoughts and precise methods.

His mind, though brilliant, often became a battlefield of overthinking – ideas clashing, doubts growing like wild vines.

One morning, standing by his window with the city's hum below, Elias made a decision:

If his mind was a garden, he would become its engineer.

He created a simple daily ritual:

Each morning, he wrote down one positive, empowering belief.

Each evening, he challenged a single limiting though that no longer served him.

Some mornings were easy; some nights were harder.

Doubts whispered louder on certain days, but Elias stayed committed.

Over time, his inner world changed.

Where chaos once reigned, clarity took root.

His mind became an elegant architecture of strength – not perfect, but alive, conscious and deeply resilient.

Takeaway: Structured Mind (Elias' Path)

"Structured minds thrive on rhythm and clarity.

Plant one belief each morning.

Challenge one doubt each night.

Over time, a strong inner architecture will rise."

Journey Two: Selene – The Silent Gardener

Selene lived closer to rivers and woods than to cities.

Her life was not a matter of strict plans or tidy schedules.

She moved with the seasons, trusted the rain, and loved the silence between her thoughts.

But even Selene knew the thorns of overthinking.

There were days when fears crept in like weeds, twisting around her heart.

Instead of fighting, she listened.

Each morning, she would sit quietly by her window.

She imagined her minds as a vast field, kissed by morning light.

She planted small thoughts of kindness, gratitude and courage – no force, just faith.

She didn't measure her growth by the day.

She trusted that beneath the surface, seeds were stirring.

Over time, the landscape within her shifted:

A garden grew – untamed yet beautiful, vibrant yet peaceful – shaped by love and gentle tending.

Takeaway: Flowing Mind (Selene's Path)

Flowing minds bloom through presence and patience.

Plant a thought – seed with trust each morning.

Nurture your inner garden gently throughout the day.

Growth will unfold like a quiet miracle."

Bringing the Two Paths Together:

While Elias built his garden with precision and design, and Selene let her grow with patience and trust, both journeys teach us a profound truth:

There is no single perfect way to tend to the mind.

Whether you find your strength in structure or in flow, the essential magic lies in the care you offer your thoughts.

Your intentions, your daily tending, your silent acts of nurturing – these shape the very soil of your future self.

Ask yourself:

What kind of gardener will you be today?

Practical exercise: Choose Your Gardening Style

Option 1: the Structured Garden (Elias' Method)

- Morning: Write one empowering belief to guide your day.

- Evening: Identify and challenged one limiting thought that surfaced.

Option 2: The Flowing Garden (Selene's Method)

- Morning: Sit quietly and visualize your mind as a blooming field.

- Throughout the day: Tend gently to your thoughts, replacing fear with love whenever needed.

You may choose one style that resonates, or blend both to create your own rhythm.

"Some gardens grow through careful hands and steady pruning.

Others bloom by trusting the rain and the quiet of the seasons.

Your mind is a living world – whether you build it brick by brick

Or sing it into blossom,

It is yours to shape.

Every thought is a seed.

Every habit, a new path through the fields of your becoming.

Tend it with love.

Grow it with hope.

Watch as the wildflowers of your mind reach for the sun."

The Key Takeaway:

"You don't eliminate overthinking by force – you outgrow it by consistently training your mind to focus, reframe, and choose clarity over confusion. Building new thought habits is about replacing loops of worry with patterns of wisdom, practiced daily through awareness, intention, and mindful repetition."

Summary: This chapter invites us into the inner worlds of Elias, an engineer entangled in endless reflection and Selene a silent gardener trapped by overthinking. Their journeys reveal that overthinking, while born from care and depth, can quietly evolve into a prison of inaction and self – doubt.

Elias believed every idea required exhaustive examination before he could act. His mind became a labyrinth of "what ifs" and "but what about," leaving his frozen at life's crossroads. Selene recalled her life's moment and countless times, never feeling they were ready for the world. Both longed for clarity, yet became lost in their pursuit of certainty.

Through their struggles, we see the heart of this chapter's lesson: overthinking strengthens the more we feed it, but every small act of choice weakens its hold. Elias turning point came when he realised that not choosing was, itself, a choice – a quiet surrender to indecision. He began asking not what was perfectly true, but what was true enough to move forward with courage.

Selene's breakthrough came when she accepted that no story is ever complete in the mind – it must be shared to grow. She created a ritual of letting go: three revisions, then release. Her thought – "Imperfect words are better than silent ones." With each honouring of this ritual, her confidence grew, and her voice found its wings.

Their intertwined journeys remind us that building new thought habits is not about silencing thought, but redirecting it toward clarity, action and peace. By becoming aware of their patterns, interrupting their loops and replacing old scripts with gentler, braver mantras, they began forging new paths through the mental forests they had long wandered.

The chapter leaves us with a quiet, powerful truth: thought habits shape our lives more than isolated choices do. Like Elias and Selene, we can step off the worn paths of worry and over – analysis and begin, one step at a time, to walk a road of clearer, kinder thinking. Change begins not with a grand epiphany, but with the courage to take a small, imperfect step forward – and to take again and again, until it becomes a way of being.

So now ask yourself: where in your life are you waiting for perfect clarity or certainty before taking action? What small, brave step could you take today, even if it feels imperfect?

Try this:

1. Identify one area where you have been overthinking or stuck in indecision.

2. Write down the smallest possible action you could take right now to move forward even if it's incomplete or imperfect.

3. Create a simple ritual to mark this action (like lighting a candle, tapping your notebook or saying a phrase aloud).

4. Take that step today. Then reflect: How did it feel to act despite uncertainty?

Each step you take builds a new path – one that leads not to perfect certainty, but to quiet courage and peaceful clarity.

Chapter 12

Creating Long – Term Mental Peace

"Strong roots grow in silence. True peace isn't something you find – it's something you plant, nurture and become."

- Rev. Lee Wolak

There is a kind of peace that does not depend on outer circumstances.

It is not found by escaping life's storms, but by learning to stand calmly within them.

In this chapter, we will explore how small daily choices can build a deep, lasting peace – a home within ourselves that nothing outside can take away.

Section 1: Planting Stillness – The foundation of Inner Calm

There was once a young man named Arun, who lived at the edge of a bustling city. Every day, he felt overwhelmed by noise – both around him and within him. His mind raced with unanswered questions, unfinished tasks, and imaginary arguments. One evening, exhausted, he wandered into a quiet park and sat beneath an old banyan tree.

An elderly gardener noticed him and approached with a gentle smile. "You look trouble, my boy," he said.

"I can't stop thinking," Arun confessed. "No matter where I go, the noise follows me."

The gardener chuckled softly. "The mind is like a wild field. If left alone, weeds of worry grow everywhere. But if you plant a single seed of stillness, and care for it daily, it will grow roots deep enough to quiet the entire field."

Intrigued, Arun asked, "How do I plant stillness?"

The gardener handed him a small sapling.

"Each day, come here and water this tree. As you nurture it, sit in silence, even for five minutes. Watch the leaves. With every moment of presence, you are also planting stillness inside yourself."

Over the weeks, Arun kept his promise. Some days his thoughts screamed louder than the silence. But as the sapling grew taller, he noticed something subtle: his inner restlessness softened. Worries didn't grip him as tightly. Clarity emerged where confusion once reigned.

Years later, the banyan tree stood strong and wide, its branches sheltering many.

And beneath its shade sat Arun, now guiding others, saying:

"Stillness isn't the absence of thought – it's the grounding of the heart. When you plant stillness, you lay the foundation of inner calm, no matter how loud the world becomes."

As Arun's sapling grew into a tree, he realised that stillness wasn't the absence of sound – it was a rooted presence beneath the noise.

Just like the banyan tree, we too can cultivate an inner stability that holds us through life's changing seasons.

"Peace comes from within. Do not seek it without." – Buddha

Exercise 1: The Five-Minute Stillness Practice

Before you begin, remember:

"Silence is the language of God; all else is poor translation." – Rumi

Sit quietly, set a time for five minutes, and watch your breath. If your mind wanders, gently return to your breathing. Let each inhale reminds you that you are here, each exhale that you can let go.

Reflection question: What did silence teach you today?

Exercise 2: Create Your "Stillness Space"

As Arun's banyan tree became a living symbol of peace, so too can a simple corner in your home hold sacredness:

"The quieter you become, the more you can hear." – Ram Dass

Decorate your space with a candle, a meaningful object, or an image that reminds you of inner peace. Let this place invite you to return to yourself daily.

Reflection question: How did your stillness space affect your emotions today?

Exercise 3: The "Tree – Watching" Mindfulness Walk

Watching a tree teaches patience, presence and rootedness:

"Be like a tree and let the dead leaves drop." - Rumi

Spend 5-10 minutes observing a tree. Notice its quiet strength, its movement without resistance. Practice letting your own thoughts fall away, like leaves.

Reflection Question: What did you notice in the tree that reflects something inside you?

Exercise 4: Stillness Journal Prompt

At the end of each day, return to your journal:

"Within you there is a stillness and a sanctuary to which you can retreat at any time."

- Hermann Hesse

Write:

- Where did I find stillness today?

- Where did I lose it?

- How can I return to it tomorrow?

Stillness is not a destination but a seed planted daily. Over time, it grows roots so deep that even the strongest winds cannot shake your peace.

"In the midst of movement and chaos, keep stillness inside of you."

- Deepak Chopra

Section 2: Quieting the Inner Noise – Releasing the Rush of Thoughts

Our minds have been trained to fill every empty space with noise: worries, to do lists, judgements, fears.

But peace begins when we stop believing every thought that passes through us.

In this section, you will learn simple ways to soften the noise and create space for calmness to naturally rise.

Let's begin: There is saying – **"The loudest noise is often inside our own heads."**

For many of us, the rush of thoughts feels like an unstoppable river – racing from one worry to another, replaying past conversations, planning future scenarios, and filling every quiet moment with inner chatter.

But what if we could step out of that rush, even for a moment? What if quiet wasn't the absence of sound, but the presence of peace?

Let me tell you a story.

Story: The Architect's Dilemma

Ethan was a brilliant architect, known for his sharp mind and flawless designs. But inside, he was drowning. Every night, he lay in bed and many thoughts were going on in his head, his mind spinning: "Did I calculate that beam's load right? Will the client approve the revisions? What if the project fails? What if they replace me?"

During the day, Ethan looked composed. But internally, he was locked in a battle with his thoughts – each one louder, faster and more urgent than the last. His work suffered. His relationships frayed. He couldn't focus anymore because his mind never rested.

One afternoon, his mentor, an old architect named Clara, invited him to a café. She noticed his distracted gaze and restless tapping.

"Ethan," she said gently, "When was the last time you let your mind be quiet?"

He frowned. "I can't. If I stop thinking, I will fall behind. I'll make mistakes."

Clara smiled. "Ah. You think that thinking harder is the solution. But it's not more thinking you need- it's more space between the thoughts."

She handed him a small stone from her pocket. "Take this," she said. "Sit somewhere peaceful. Every time a thought comes, imagine setting it down beside you like a stone. Don't fight it, don't analyse it – just place it down. And sit with what remains."

That evening, Ethan tried. At first, the thoughts came relentlessly. But slowly, as he imagined setting each one down – a missed deadline, a criticism, a fear – he began to feel lighter.

There was a strange, unfamiliar quiet. Not empty, but peaceful. For the first time in years, he slept deeply.

The next morning, something surprising happened: clarity. He solved a design problem that had stumped him for weeks – not by forcing the solution, but by creating space for it to emerge.

Explanation:

Ethan's story shows a truth that many of us overlook: sometimes the answer, the clarity, and the relief we seek can only arise in stillness. When the mind is noisy, wisdom gets drowned out. Quieting the inner noise isn't about suppressing thoughts or making the mind blank – it's about releasing the compulsion to chase every thought and letting them flow without attachment.

This doesn't happen automatically; it's a practice. But each moment of quiet opens a doorway to peace, insight and renewal.

Practical Exercise: The Stone Practice

Objective: To create space between thoughts and experience inner quiet by symbolically releasing mental clutter.

Instructions:

1. Find a quiet place where you won't be disturbed for 10 -15 minutes. Sit comfortably.

2. Place a small bowl or tray next to you. Gather a handful of small objects (stones, coins, buttons)

3. Close your eyes. Begin to notice the thoughts that arise. Each time a thought comes, mentally name it (e.g. "deadline worry," "argument replay," "future fear").

4. For each thought, pick up one object and gently place it in the bowl, symbolising setting the thought down.

5. After placing each object, return to stillness. Notice the space that follows.

Continue until you've placed all objects.

6. When finished, sit quietly for a few more moments, observing the silence you have created.

7. Reflect: How did it feel to set thoughts down? Did any emotions or insights arise?

Reflection Takeaway:

Each thought you "set down" is a reminder that you don't have to carry everything at once. By practicing symbolic release, you create inner space where clarity and calm can emerge. Over time, this practice can help to reduce mental clutter and deepen your capacity for mindful presence.

Section 3: Returning to Centre – Making Peace Your Default

Moments of peace are precious, but what transforms life is making them regular.

Like a river carving stone, small daily rituals of calmness shape the very structure of your mind.

Here, we'll create simple, joyful "anchors" that help you return to your centre – again and again – until it becomes natural.

In today's fast – moving world, we often believe peace is something we must "earn" by finishing tasks, solving problems, or fixing every detail of our lives. But true peace – the kind that steadies the heart and clears the mind – is not something external.

It's a practice: the art of returning to your centre, again and again, no matter the storms around you.

This section offers you a practical, story driven exercise designed for modern life struggles and busy daily routines. It is designed to help you build peace as your default state – a quiet strength inside that you can always return to.

Story: The Archer and the Storm

There was once a master archer named Kael who lived on the edge of a mountain village.

Known for his unmatched precision, Kael never missed a mark. But one year, a great storm rolled across the mountains. The winds howled, the earth trembled, and the villagers became restless, seeking Kael's calm.

But Kael himself was shaken. His hands trembled when he picked up his bow. He had always relied on perfect stillness and clear skies to steady his aim – now, the storm mocked his control. Day after day, Kael fought to regain his calm, but the harder he tried, the more anxious he became.

One evening, an old monk passing through the village stopped to watch Kael practice. Seeing Kael's frustration, the monk smiled gently and said,

"You do not need to control the wind, only yourself."

The monk invited Kael to sit quietly in the storm, without his bow, without aiming, just breathing. At first, Kael resisted. But slowly, as he sat in silence, he realised something profound:

"Centring himself did not mean stopping the storm; it meant finding peace inside, no matter the storm outside."

From that day on, Kael became not just a master archer but a master of returning to centre. Whether in chaos or calm, peace became his default– a home inside himself.

Practical Exercise: Your Inner Anchor

1. **Find your Quiet Spot:**

Sit comfortably in a chair or on the floor.

Close your eyes and take three slow, deep breaths.

2. **Notice the "Storm":**

Let your mind wander to the things stressing you right now. Notice the racing thoughts, the tension, the worries – don't push them away. Just observe them like clouds passing.

3. **Return to Centre:**

Now, gently shift your attention to your breath – the natural rhythm of air moving in and out. Feel your feet on the ground or your body's weight where it rests. Say silently:

"I am here. I am safe. I return to centre."

4. Anchor Phrase:

Pick a personal word or phrase (like "peace," "steady," or "calm") and repeat it with each exhale for the next 2-3 minutes. Let it be your mental anchor, bringing you back whenever your mind drifts.

Refection Takeaway

- Peace is not the absence of challenges; it's the presence of inner anchor.

- When you practice returning to your centre, you train your nervous system to make peace your default, even when life pulls you off balance.

- Over time, this builds emotional resilience – the ability to face storms without losing your ground.

- Returning to your centre means unplugging regularly to ground yourself in real space and time.

Section 4: Growing Stability – Practices That Build Deep Calm

True stability is not about controlling life, but about building a mind strong enough to flow with it.

Simple practices – breathing, walking mindfully, journaling emotions – are the stones that create a peaceful path beneath your feet.

Each step you take here will strengthen the quiet strength within you.

In a world that constantly pulls us in every direction, deep calm is not something we stumble upon – it is something we cultivate. Growing stability means grounding ourselves so that life's external storms no longer shake us internally. It's about practices that root us in presence, patience and resilience.

This section will offer you a practical, story driven exercise that will help you to be patient and silent in life at any situation or ups and downs.

Story 1: The Mountain Monk's Breath Technique

In the range of Himalayas, a monk lived named Tenzin used to practice meditative breathing every morning. When he was asked how he stayed so calm during landslides, avalanches, and harsh winters, he smiled and said,

"The mountain teaches me: storms come and go, but the breath remains."

He explained that just as the mountain stands steady while the weather changes, his breath anchored him through life's ups and downs.

Practice: Mountain Breath Exercise

- Sit upright, hands resting gently on your knees.

- Inhale slowly for 4 counts, hold for 4 counts, exhale for 6 counts.

- As you breath, silently say:

"I am steady like the mountain; storms pass over me."

- Repeat for 5 minutes.

Reflection Takeaway:

Your breath is your anchor. By returning to it, you remind yourself that you are bigger than your worries. The breath teaches you calm endurance. Let's see the next story.

Story 2: The Potter's Hands

In a small village there lived a young woman named Aya worked as a potter. One day, a visitor watched her work the clay arts and asked,

"How do you stay so focused and peaceful while shaping these delicate pieces?"

Aya replied,

"My hands teach my mind. When my hands move slowly and mindfully, my thoughts slow down too."

She knew that through gentle, rhythmic work, she calmed her heart.

Practice: Mindful Hands Ritual

- Choose a slow, repetitive task: washing dishes, folding clothes, watering plants.

- As you perform it, focus entirely on the texture, movement, and rhythm.

- If your mind wanders, gently return your attention to your hands.

Reflection Takeaway

Your body can lead your mind into calm. By engaging in mindful, physical tasks, you train your brain to rest.

Story 3: The Lighthouse Keeper's Watch

On a rugged coastline, an old lighthouse keeper named Eron tended the light every night.

He said,

"I cannot control the waves or the storms, but I can keep the light steady."

Even when chaos raged outside, he found peace knowing his small, steady duty mattered.

Practice: Steady Focus Drill

- Pick one small daily task (like journaling or tidying a corner) and commit to doing it at the same time every day.

- Focus on consistency over perfection.

- Remind yourself: "This is my light, I keep it steady."

Reflection Takeaway:

Calm grows through small, consistent acts. Even when life is turbulent, you can ground yourself by tending your own light.

Story 4: The Oak Tree's Roots

There was a small village where a farmer lived with his daughter. The farmer once told his daughter,

"In the storm, weak trees fall, but the oak stands because its roots run deep."

He taught her to deepen her roots by connecting with family, values and her inner sense of meaning – not shallow distractions.

Practice: Root Connection Check – In

- Take 10 minutes to reflect on:

  Who or what gives you a sense of deep connection?

  What values or beliefs ground you?

- Write these down and keep them visible (on your desk or phone background)

Reflection Takeaway:

True calm comes from being deeply rooted – not in fleeting pleasures, but in your core connections and values.

Final Reflection:

Building deep calm is not about escaping life's challenges; it's about growing inner stability that hold you steady through them. Like mountains, clay, light and oak trees, you too can practice patience, breath, mindfulness, consistency, and connection.

If you practice even one of these each day, over time you will cultivate a calm that's unshakable.

You have already planted the seeds of patience, breath awareness, mindful action, consistency and purpose. Remember calm is not a destination – it's a practice. You can return to these exercises anytime if life feels overwhelming.

In the next section we will explore about the trust that finally brings the success provided you should have trust.

Section 5: Trusting the Process – The Bamboo and the Gardener

Growth often feels invisible – until one day, it is undeniable.

Patience is not weakness; it is faith in the unseen roots we are nurturing every day.

Through a small story of a patience gardener and a stubborn bamboo seed, you will see why your quiet efforts matter for more than you realise.

Story: The Bamboo Farmer's Patience

In a small village of Japan, there lived an old farmer named Kenji, known for his calm nature. While others rushed to grow rice or vegetables, Kenji quietly tended a small patch of Moso bamboo.

People laughed at him because for four long years, the bamboo showed no signs of growth. Every morning, Kenji watered the plants and fertilized what looked like an empty patch of soil.

"Why do you waste your time?" the villagers mocked.

"You could grow something useful!"

But Kenji simply smiled and continued.

Then, in the fifth year, something miraculous happened. The bamboo shot up more than 80 feet in just six weeks.

What the villagers hadn't seen was that during those four "empty" years, the bamboo was growing an invisible root system, spreading deep and wide beneath the surface, anchoring itself so it could rise tall without toppling in the wind.

Kenji's secret was not just in the bamboo, but in his own mind-set. He cultivated patience, consistency, and faith – practicing a quiet, deep and calm no matter what others said or how slow things seemed.

Practice: Root – Building Routine

To grow your own deep stability, practice this Root – Building Routine each day:

1. Morning Grounding (5 minutes)

Before you pick up phone or start work, sit quietly and place both your feet on the ground. Take 10 slow, conscious breaths. With each inhale, imagine drawing calm energy from the earth. With each exhale, release tension.

2. Daily Patience Affirmation

Repeat softly:

"I am building roots even when growth is not visible. Patience is my power."

3. Evening Reflection (5 minutes)

At the end of day, ask yourself:

- Where did I practice patience today?

- What small action today is strengthening my foundation for tomorrow?

Write your answer in a journal. This reflection will help you reinforce the sense that you are growing, even when you can't yet see the result.

Reflection Takeaway

Calm is not passive; it's a living strength you nourish daily. Like bamboo, true growth often happens underground – in the quiet moments, the steady routines, the invisible acts of patience. Trust that by tending to your roots, you are preparing yourself to rise tall when the time is right.

Bonus Exercise: "Plant Your Bamboo" Ritual

Title: Plant Your Bamboo – A Quiet Commitment to Your Growth

Instruction for the Readers:

Today, take a small symbolic action to honour your silent inner growth.

You can either:

- Plant an actual seed in a pot or garden or

- Write down one word (like "patience," "peace," "trust," or "growth") on a piece of paper and bury it under a small stone, candle or book you love.

This is not about the plant or the paper.

It's about you making a quiet, sacred promise to yourself:

"I trust the roots I am building, even when I cannot see them yet."

Every time you see the growing the plant or remember the hidden word, you will remember:

Your inner peace is growing too – silently, patiently, powerfully.

Daily Affirmation for Long – Term Mental Peace

"I trust the quiet work happening within me.

I am patient, I am rooted, I am already growing."

Quick Tips for Using It:

Dear readers you can follow these

- Repeat it once each morning and once each night before going on the bed for the next 30 days.

- Whisper it silently to yourself whenever you feel impatient or discouraged.

- Even write it on a sticky note near your desk, mirror or journal.

It becomes a soft, steady companion for your journey into deeper peace.

"May you have the patience of the bamboo, the faith of the unseen seed, and the joy of knowing that true peace has already begun inside you."

Conclusion

"When the mind is silent, the soul speaks – and its voice is always peace."

- Ancient Wisdom

Overthinking is not your enemy – it is your untrained mind trying to protect you. It whispers questions, replays memories, imagines future, and seeks control, all in the name of safety.

But as we have discovered in these pages, when left unchecked, this mental noise can drown out your clarity, creativity, and confidence.

You have journeyed through the roots of overthinking – its psychological mechanisms, emotional triggers, and cognitive distortions.

You've seen how it affects love, decision making, ambition, and inner peace. You've explored ancient wisdom, modern science, and real human experiences. And most importantly, you've gained tools – not just to reduce the noise, but to transform the silence that follows into strength.

The truth is this: Your mind is not a battlefield. It's a garden. Overthinking may have filled it with weeds, but now you know how to clear space for clarity to grow.

A resilient mind is not one that breaks, but one that bends – learning to grow stronger in the face of every storm.

Let your reflections guide you, not trap you.

Let your thoughts be companions, not captors.

Let your silence be sacred, not suffocating.

Every moment of awareness, every breath of mindfulness, and every step away from rumination is a step toward your true self – present, peaceful, and powerful.

This is not the end. This is a beginning.

The beginning of a quieter mind. A clearer heart.

And a life led not by fear, but by insight.

Your Final Reflection Ritual

Take a moment now – before you close this book – to connect with yourself in silence.

3 – Step Reflection Practice

i)   Sit in stillness for 3-5 minutes. No distractions. Just observe your breath.

ii) Write down one recurring thought you've been overthinking lately.

iii) Answer this prompt honestly:

> "If I stopped trying to control this thought and simply trusted myself,

> What would I do differently right now?"

Let the answer guide your next step – not with pressure, but with peace.

Takeaway Mantra

"I am not my overthinking. I am the

Awareness beneath it – calm, wise, and free."

Keep this mantra with you. Write it. Repeat it.

Live it.

And whenever the noise returns, remember:

You have already begun the journey back to clarity.

Cheers!

Gratitude Towards Readers

Dear Readers,

First and foremost, I would like to give you special thanks for giving time to read this book. You could have chosen any other book, but you took mine, and I totally appreciate this.

I hope it will elevate your life and transform your world. You might have got at least a few actionable insights that will have a positive impact on your day to day life.

Thanks for your support to my work, and I love your decision to purchase this book and implement the practical exercises to get instant results that will take you from mental chaos to inner peace.

Full Book Summary

Introduction: Key Takeaways

Overthinking is a silent burden of the modern mind – understanding it is the first step toward clarity. The mind holds immense power, but when left unchecked, it can become our greatest enemy. This book is a journey, not a quick fix – offering both insight and practical tools to transform overthinking into clear, confident action.

Part 1: Understanding Overthinking

Chapter 1: What Is Overthinking? – Key Takeaways

Overthinking involves repetitive, unproductive thought loops – often rooted in fear, uncertainty, or the need for control.

It drains emotional energy and hijacks focus, leading to indecision, stress and procrastination.

Overthinking disguises itself as intelligence or caution but often prevents action.

Chapter 2: The Psychology behind Overthinking – Key Takeaways

Overthinking is linked to cognitive distortions (e.g. catastrophizing, all or nothing thinking) and hyperactivity in the brain's Default Mode Network.

Historical and fictional case studies show how overthinking has real – life consequences.

Our brain, while trying to protect us, can create self – sabotaging thought patterns when left untrained.

Chapter 3: The Impact of Overthinking on Your Life – Key Takeaways

Overthinking damages relationships, weakens decision – making, and reduces life satisfaction.

Chronic rumination is linked to anxiety, insomnia, and emotional burnout.

Recognizing its impact helps you to treat overthinking not as a personality trait, but as a solvable mental pattern.

Part 2: Identifying Your Overthinking Patterns

Chapter 4: Recognizing Your Mental Traps – Key Takeaways

Mental traps such as perfectionism, fear of failure, and needing certainty often trigger overthinking.

Becoming aware of these traps is key to breaking free from them.

Self – awareness is the foundation of change.

Chapter 5: Triggers and Patterns of Overthinking

Overthinking is often triggered by specific environments, people, or emotional states.

Identifying your unique triggers allows you to respond rather than react.

Tracking patterns helps you spot overthinking early and apply mental redirection.

Chapter 6: Tools for Self – Assessment – Key Takeaways

Self – assessment tools (like thought logs and emotional mapping) help uncover hidden thought loops.

Journal and self – inquiry provide insight into the root cause of your rumination.

Awareness precedes action: you can't change what you don't first observe.

Part 3: Practical Solutions to Overcome Overthinking

Chapter 7: Mindfulness Techniques to Control Overthinking – Key Takeaways

Mindfulness trains your brain to return to the present instead of spiralling into "what ifs."

Simple practices like breath awareness, body scanning, and mindful walking create mental space.

Consistent mindfulness rewires the brain for clarity and calm.

Chapter 8: Practical Exercises for Mental Clarity – Key Takeaways

Grounding techniques, visualizations, and structured decision – making reduce mental clutter.

Creating a "mental parking lot" helps separate action – worthy thoughts from noise.

Clarity doesn't come from more thinking, but from better thinking.

Chapter 9: Cognitive Behavioural Tools to Disrupt Overthinking – Key Takeaways

CBT tools like thought – challenging and reframing disrupt cognitive distortion.

You learn to examine thoughts logically rather than emotionally.

Shifting perspective is a powerful antidote to repetitive worry.

Part 4: Transforming Overthinking into Clarity

Chapter 10: Developing a Resilient Mind set – Key Takeaways

Resilience means bending with stress, not breaking under it.

Building mental resilience involves embracing discomfort, failure, and uncertainty as growth tools.

A resilient mind redirects overthinking into productive thought, learning and forward motion.

Chapter 11: Building New Thought Habits – Key Takeaways

Thought habits are changeable – they are just mental grooves you have walked too often.

Repetition of new habits (affirmations, journaling, and decisive action) creates cognitive momentum.

The brain learns through doing, not wishing – habit is a practice of becoming.

Chapter 12: Creating Long – Term Mental Peace – Key Takeaways

Mental peace comes not from controlling life, but from accepting its flow.

Practices like gratitude, solitude, nature immersion, and spiritual reflection deepen calm.

Long – term peace is possible when you stop resisting the mind and start befriending it.

About the Author

Arvind Kaiwartya is a self - help author, teacher, deep thinker, and guide for those navigate the complexities of the modern mind, who has inspired thousand and thousand of students to transform their lives through the power of positive thinking time to time.

With year of experience in the field of teaching, Arvind has gained recognition for his attractive classes that hepl students and people to unlock their potential, overcome obstacle and achieve goal. His simple and approachable style of teaching along with motivation has given him a new recognition.

Being a teacher his mission is to educate people to live their life happily. Passionate about blending psychology, philosophy, and spiritual insight, Arvind Kaiwartya writes to help others find clarity in chaos and peace in overthinking.

Master Your Mind is the first in the Mind Mirror Series - books crafted for thoughtful souls seeking real change.

May I Ask You For A Favor

First, I want to thank you for reading this book. You could have chosen any other book, but you took mine, and I appreciate this. I hope you have at least a few actionable insights that will positively impact your daily life.

Can I ask for 30 seconds more of your time?

I'd love it if you could leave a review of the book. That will help me grow my readership by encouraging folks to take a chance on my books.

Keeping it straight - reviews are the lifeblood of any author.

It will take less than a minute of your time but will tremendously help me reach out to more people.

If you liked this book, please consider posting an honest review on your preferred retailer. And I'd love to see your review. Thanks for your support.

www.ingramcontent.com/pod-product-compliance
Lightning Source LLC
Chambersburg PA
CBHW051241130726
47988CB00001B/439